Fishing Aroun
Bristol Channel

Fishing Around the Bristol Channel

Mike Smylie with Simon Cooper

For Ann and Moe

First published 2011

The History Press
The Mill, Brimscombe Port
Stroud, Gloucestershire, GL5 2QG
www.thehistorypress.co.uk

British Library Cataloguing in Publication Data.
A catalogue record for this book is available from the British Library.

ISBN 978 0 7524 5792 5

Typesetting and origination by The History Press
Printed in Great Britain
Manufacturing managed by Jellyfish Print Solutions Ltd

CONTENTS

INTRODUCTION

The Severn Sea – better known as the Bristol Channel – has fascinated me for many years for, though it was once one of the busiest shipping lanes in the country, it seems to some extent to be shrouded in mystery and thus to be avoided. Yet Bristol, its chief maritime terminus, was once the second-largest port in Britain whilst the shores support dozens of communities engaged in maritime activities. Fishing, pilotage, life-saving, smuggling, the coastal trade and even a spot of wrecking if some reports are to be believed – it has it all, coupled up with the second-highest tidal height in the world.

I guess part of the problem is that it seems a bit of a misnomer, this 'channel' bit. The word channel is associated with a piece of water leading through to somewhere, such as the St George's or English Channels, and not as a sort of Norwegian fjord or Scottish loch. In truth a channel is a stream of water and this the Bristol Channel is, as well as being a channel leading to Bristol. With the many rivers flowing out – those numerous tributaries flowing through the South Wales valleys, the great Severn and Wye from mid-Wales, the Avon from the east, the waterways draining the Somerset Levels and the outflows from lofty Exmoor including the Taw and Torridge – and the strong tides, it is a channel in the proper sense. Yet it remains a seaway many boatmen and yachtsmen dread.

I was first encouraged of the positive aspects of the area when reading Brian Waters' trilogy, especially *The Bristol Channel* which was published in the year of my birth. Somehow he had unlocked some of the magic and mystery in a wonderful way. Since then little has been written about it as a whole. John Gilman's *Exmoor's Maritime Heritage* has to be the finest investigation of those few ports along the southern part, whilst Tony James' *Yankee Jack Sails Again* conjures up the sort of sentiment about the south-west that the blurb on the cover says when he visits the forgotten ports on his way down the coast from Watchet to Cornwall, but the story is written in a jaunty sort of way. Amongst the ports he visited were a few no longer present such as Lilstock, Highbridge and Hartland Quay where nearly all signs of human presence by way of quays, jetties and warehouses are gone, vanished through the ravages of the sea. But that's another story. Nevertheless he paints a vivid picture of the times when the sea was the only link between communities, and writes with a vigour for the subject, different as it is to Brian Waters'. The ports and coves of South Wales figure in various publications, though none jump immediately to mind. Everyone mentions the fishing though no one really explores it, for the Bristol Channel is regarded as an area largely being devoid of fish. As Brian

Waters says, Ilfracombe, once the herring capital of the Bristol Channel, has hardly seen a herring in eighty years. Today there may be some truth in the fact that fish avoid the area, though there still remain some who make their living from it. James summed up much of what remains of British commercial fishing culture today during his visit to St Ives: 'Today there are more fishermen and fishing boats in paintings in St Ives' forty galleries and craft centres than go to sea.' All around the coast, from Cornish quaint villages on the edge of the sea to Scottish lochs overwhelmed by fish farms, it seems it is only nostalgia and art that combine to keep fishing alive. A century ago it was a very different thing, for each coast-based community living on the edge of the Bristol Channel, as any other shore, gained some benefit from the fruits of the sea. In fact, more so than in other parts of the British coast. Here, in these pages, we glimpse a small part of that story.

So what and where exactly is the Bristol Channel? Edgar March, author of various seminal books on British fishing craft, wrote in *Inshore Craft of Great Britain* (vol. 2) that the:

> Bristol Channel opens between Hartland Point on the south and St Ann's Head, some 48 miles distant to the north. The shores of the channel now run eastward for about 100 miles, gradually converging until they meet the river Severn pouring out its waters gathered over a length of 180 miles. This funnel shape, and the swift tidal movements meeting the fierce current from inland, kick up vicious seas...

That seems to be enough, though it is these vicious seas that have moulded much of the people and, especially, their vessels and the places they shelter within on this wind-torn stretch of water facing the full brunt of the Atlantic. I'm reminded of what many a salty sailor has been heard to lament: 'I don't bloody want to sail there ever again.' But then, there are those in Bristol Docks, or Watchet, or Cardiff that think the opposite. To them the Channel is a challenge, as well as their home. A bit of a beat out, yes, but an easy ride home, especially in a well-founded boat. To those who fished these waters and seashores, it too was home. The only difference being they had no choice.

In recent years boatbuilders of the Bristol Channel and the West Country have been foremost in the building of so-called 'eco boats' which are replicas of older types. St Ives (out of the area but not by far) has two 'jumbos' as we write, whilst the Clovelly picaroon is well established. In Milford the building of a traditional Tenby Lugger has just commenced as this goes to press; three types then that suggest a return to values that fishermen of a previous generation adhered to. Fishing under sail, practised by the Falmouth oyster-fishers since anyone can remember, and before, might be due for a comeback with a premium paid for what would in effect be carbon-zero fish. We will see.

With regard to the preparation of this book, the most sincerest of thanks must go to Stephen Perham, Brendan and Adrian Sellick, John Nash of the Watchet Boat Museum, the North Devon Maritime Museum and Nicola Caldwell of the Scolton Manor Museum. All uncredited photographs were taken by Mike Smylie.

Mike Smylie, January 2011

1

THE LAST HERRING FISHER OF CLOVELLY?

Willie McSporran of the Island of Gigha, off Western Scotland, famously had something in the region of twelve jobs including postman and undertaker. Although he doesn't deliver the post nor look after the dead, as harbour master, boatman, lobster potter, lifeboat coxswain, harbour repair worker, tripping boat operator, unofficial bodyguard, shopkeeper and general factotum, as well as pretty much the last of the herring fishermen, Stephen Perham of Clovelly must surely be somewhere comparable. He's also a keen local maritime historian and has been collecting data on Clovelly's fishery for a number of years.

I first met Stephen in the autumn of 2004 whilst recording for Radio 4's *Food Programme*, when he took presenter Sheila Dillon, producer Margaret Collins and myself out in his small fibreglass rowboat one perfect December evening, just after dark, for a spot of fishing a couple of hundred yards from the harbour, along the shore. We put a few nets down and half an hour later were hauling in our catch of a few bucketfuls of the silver darlings. Once back upon the harbour wall a few customers arrived to buy some of the fish whilst others we took to the Red Lion Hotel for the chef to cook for our evening meal. Fresh, small and flavoursome from a simple baking in the hotel's oven, they were perfect, delicate and almost unsurpassable. Since then we've met on numerous occasions, as well as during the annual Herring Festival Clovelly holds in November, at which time I've smoked some of his freshly landed herring which subsequently turned into delicate-tasting bloaters and golden kippers.

Stephen has been out herring fishing since before he was a teenager, when he would join his father. He remembers being woken at dawn to help his mother and aunt shake

Clovelly Harbour from above in autumn with the Red Lion Hotel on the left. Most of these boats were motorised by this time. (Courtesy of Petros Kounouklas)

Boats in the harbour, *c*.1950. Clovelly fishing boats are registered in Bideford (BD), although these are motor boats. A picarooner lies on the beach by the pier. (Mike Smylie Collection)

out the nets after the boats had come in. When the nationwide ban came in 1977 he was twelve and when fishing was once again permitted seven years later his father was dead. But fortunately his father had passed on some of his knowledge in recognising the natural appearances of the herring – the oil on the water, the way the seabirds behaved and even watching the natural predators. Stephen was able to continue the family tradition.

Clovelly has long been renowned for the quality of its herring as supported by Thomas Westcote in 1630 and Charles Harper nearly three centuries later. In between the fishing had been intermittent for, as elsewhere, the herring is notoriously fickle, appearing for years on the trot in one particular place and suddenly abandoning it for another, only to return without notice years later. Such were, and still are to a certain extent, the mixed fortunes of generations of herring fishermen. Now, though, things are different and more often than not it is the market for the fish that is fickle. With demand low for them, it is only Steve who perseveres and ventures out whenever the weather is favourable, although a couple of the other fishermen might attempt the odd trip out if things look really good, his brother Tom being one of these. But even that hasn't changed. According to Mr Frank Vine, he remembered the picarooners coming in to Clovelly 'loaded down to the point of sinking, and even then they'd had to cut away three or four nets of their eleven' and 'donkeys forever toiling up the hill with a maund of herring on each side', a maund being a basket holding a mease of herring (612 fish). Others from the hinterland would come down with a cart and horse to take away a load to hawk about. Late in the week no one hawked, it seems, so at best a farmer would come down for a cartload to use as manure, and 'if that failed, the men would cheerfully load them into the picarooners and row them out to sea to dump them overboard again'. That gives a whole new dimension to today's problem of discards!

Crazy Kate's Cottage in the late nineteenth century. This was once the home of Kate Lyall, who died in 1830, demented after the loss of her husband in the bay. Today it's the family home of Stephen Perham. (Courtesy of Stephen Perham)

Phil and Geffe Dunn emptying the herring nets from their picarooner on the beach in 1917. The Red Lion is in the background. (Courtesy of Stephen Perham)

Outside the Red Lion in the late 1880s. On the left is William Bates and next to him is Tom Pengelly, master-mariner, fisherman and lifeboat coxswain with the local cobbler Alexander Pedlar wearing the bowler hat. From the right is fisherman Robert Badcock with his son Frank on his knee, John Whitfield, another master-mariner, Stephen Headon, fisherman, and William Prince, also a fisherman. (Courtesy of Stephen Perham)

This information from sixty-eight-year-old Frank Vine was recorded by Vernon Carr Boyle of Trumpington, Cambridgeshire in the 1930s and '40s, the date for the previously mentioned quotes being November 1948. Boyle was well known to members of the Society for Nautical Research, which at that time was keenly gathering information on vernacular British craft under the auspices of the Coastal and River Craft Sub-Committee. Their work ultimately led to much of the information we have today on working craft and the drawings of many of these vessels, by P.J. Oke under the committee's instructions, lie in the Science Museum. However Boyle's work on the Clovelly herring boats largely went unpublished, possibly due to his untimely and sudden death in June 1954, though he did publish several articles.

Clovelly's fishing boats were of some 5 to 6 tons in the second half of the eighteenth century, of which there were about 100. They were 20ft clinker-built open boats with a square mainsail and sprit mizzen, although some appear to have been lug-rigged. As often as not these boats were propelled by oars alone, especially when fishing. Around 1800 there were about sixty boats in the harbour and in 1839 the harbourmaster recorded fifty small boats, six large boats and another sixteen 'engaged in the taking of large fish'. The latter seemingly were the long-boomers, of which we will learn more later.

We don't know the date upon which the first carvel-built herring boat first appeared in Clovelly; but that such a type existed we do know. Although Oke never managed to get to Clovelly to measure a boat – he also died suddenly on his motorcycle – Boyle did measure up the *Pearl* in Fremington Pill on the river Taw between August 1933 and January 1934, and from his measurements he produced a rough lines plan, the only one in existence.

Right: Fisherman Frank Badcock. He and fellow fisherman William Harding were drowned whilst out fishing on 1 January 1919. Frank survived being at sea during the First World War only to succumb to the sea the following year. His father Robert, in the previous photograph, committed suicide by hanging himself. (Courtesy of Stephen Perham)

Below: The women of the family always helped with the clearing of the nets once the boat had returned. Here Jack Headon, on the right, and Fred, on the left, are seen with Jack's daughters shaking the herring onto the pebbles in 1917. (Courtesy of Stephen Perham)

Nets drying upon the pier alongside the Red Lion. Nets were treated regularly by 'barking', immersing them in a solution of hot water and 'cutch', the resin from the Indian Acacia tree, to enable them to last in the salt water. Drying also helped retard the disintegration process. (Courtesy of Stephen Perham)

The Clovelly Herring boats, as they've become known, were 20ft as well so presumably not too altered from the older vessels. They were lug-rigged and seemed only to work during the autumn herring season. Most fishermen had a smaller ladging boat, similar to Bucks Mills Ledge boats of which we will hear more later. Some also had a share in a bigger trawler. *Pearl* was the largest herring boat built at 24ft and almost the last, it seems. Built in 1883 at the boatyard below the bridge at Bideford – it has been suggested the owner was Dick Blackmore – it seemed that the days of the bigger herring boats were almost over. By that time Pool Quay had started to silt up and the big boats were constrained by the tide. To counter this the first smaller boat was introduced in 1880, the hull of which was modelled on the herring boats but, at about 16ft, was much easier to push down to the water's edge at low tide and could return back at any stage of the tide. Thus they quickly multiplied and were the first back with the catch. The owners of the big boats termed them 'picarooners' from the Spanish meaning 'sea robber' or 'pirate', although no one seems to know why they used a Spanish term!

An apprentice in the yard at the time of *Pearl*'s construction was Jim Whitefield and he later moved to Clovelly to build picarooners and smaller punts on his own count, working from what is now a seafood shop belonging to Stephen's brother, a few steps up from the harbour, until retiring about 1925. Clovelly had several boatbuilders resident,

Fisherman Oscar Abbot inspecting his nets drying upon the pier. His family were originally Bude fishermen and Oscar is remembered as being one of the best herring fishermen. He died about 1970. (Courtesy of Stephen Perham)

'Bringing to a net.' This is the setting up of the drift-net at which the net itself is attached to the head rope. A drift-net floats on the surface of the sea so that the net is suspended downwards though the fisherman uses his local knowledge to ensure it is kept in water deep enough so that it does not foul the seabed. The net belonged to the Dunn family who also owned the *Teazer*. (Courtesy of Stephen Perham)

The *Pearl* at Fremington where she eventually rotted away. She was skippered by Jack Harris. (Courtesy of Vernon Boyle)

A seemingly peaceful view of the village with a picarooner sitting alongside. (Courtesy of Stephen Perham)

Shaking the herring from the nets. Note the number of boats landing on the beach. (Mike Smylie Collection)

A good net of herring in the 1960s. This is Si, Clive and Norman Headon again clearing their catch. The children are joining in and the boy on the left, Ticker Glover, is obviously curious about a herring! The other boy on the extreme right is Chris Searles. (Courtesy of Stephen Perham)

Tom Waters being there until moving to Appledore about 1855, and Peter Mills. Before that, in 1804, a man referred to as Mr Barrow had three shipwrights and four apprentices working from his Clovelly yard.

Luckily Boyle was able to talk to Whitefield and others who had known the *Pearl*. Built for the owner of a fish and chip shop in Barnstaple, she was later sold to Captain Fred Prance who was originally from nearby Peppercombe. At the time Boyle interviewed him, in 1933, he was about seventy-five years old, which puts him born somewhere about the late 1850s. When he was a boy there were nine or ten boats at Peppercombe and eighteen at Bucks Mills and his father, William Prance, had a 16ft boat, so he was brought up with boats and understood them. He therefore tells a bit about *Pearl* and its layout and obviously regarded her as a good sea boat for he recounted the time they were caught out in a gale by the Bellbuoy (which I assume is off the Bideford Bar) and had to beat home to Clovelly. Under storm lug, which was half the size of the big lug, they made Veernham and had to tack again to make home, pumping all the time for the boat took water over the quarter. The pump, incidentally, was a lever pump on the starboard quarter. The foredeck extended some 18in aft of the mast with a slide to draw back when the mast was to be lowered. On the starboard side of this was an entrance and inside the cuddy was big enough for two men to stretch out.

Lobster pot-making from withies cut from the woods above the village in the 1930s. Albert Braund is on the right with Bert Braund on the left. (Courtesy of Stephen Perham)

In the Science Museum there is a photograph of a model of the 19.2ft herring boat *Rattling Jack*, built in 1886 by Captain John Mills whose father Peter was building herring boats at Clovelly thirty years before him. The model was in fact made and lent (later presented) to the museum by Vernon Boyle in 1933. Although built for fishing, she was at the time of the Science Museum study of 1937 being used for pleasure tripping from Clovelly around the bay. However she was rose-on then, having at some time an added top strake and decking. Boyle writes that she was like a Bucks Mills boat with a foredeck extending back to the fore thwart. Her bilge plank was said to be 2.5in thick! However, in the Science Museum photo, she is 'decked forward, with wide waterways which were continued right aft'. The big dipping lug had three reefs and the tack was secured to a hook at the end of the short iron bumpkin which projected from the bow. The Beer luggers from South Devon use a similar bumpkin today.

There's still not much known about *Pearl*'s history except that sometime after Prance owned her J. Williams had her and he sold her to Jack Harris of Clovelly, another of Boyle's interviewees, this time in August 1934. Harris described the way that the two lugs were used, one for each leg of the beat home, the other meanwhile lowered. When standing close to the land the big sail was set with a reef in it. On going about and standing outwards every moment brought the boat out to bigger seas so the small mizzen lug was used. In worse weather the winter lug and storm lug might be the two. Harris

Fishermen Bert Braund, George Lamey, Stevie Headon, Fred Shackson and Jack Harris sitting atop the beach in the 1960s. (Courtesy of Stephen Perham)

reckoned this manoeuvre was 'rather special to Bideford Bay' and added that it obviated the need for dipping the lug or, as he put it, 'fetching the yard and wet sail around abaft of the mast when staying, for there is the other sail lying ready to hoist'.

Jack Harris eventually sold the boat to someone in Fremington in 1926. However, it seems that at some time prior to this, *Pearl* was cutter-rigged, being used for 'pleasure cruising and trawling, mostly at Ilfracombe and then again at Clovelly'. At Fremington she worked for seven years barging gravel in the river Taw, still under a sloop rig. Then, around 1932, she was left at Fremington Pill where it is presumed she eventually fell apart. Boyle tried to raise money for her preservation, as a paragraph in *The Times* of 1935 shows. Then it was assumed that she was the last of the Clovelly Herring boats. There's a figure standing looking into the boat in the photograph in *The Times* and I wonder whether that is Boyle himself. Another article, probably written by Boyle himself although there's no one mentioned, appeared in *The Navy* magazine in September 1935. Unfortunately, as we know, Boyle failed in his attempts to preserve the boat and now the type remains one of those extinct ones that little is known of. One little inconsistency I fail to understand is that, with *Pearl* said to be the last survivor of these boats, how come *Rattling Jack* was still being used for pleasure trips at Clovelly?

With the picarooners it is a different story, for there are about six original craft in existence. The 17ft *Faith*, belonging to and used by Stephen and vaguely famous for

Stephen's father Gordon Perham making his own lobster pots outside their house up the village. The boy is Stephen Thompson and the dog Judy. (Courtesy of Stephen Perham)

Gordon Perham in the punt with a catch of herring coming onto the beach. Note the furled mizzen sail, used to steady the boat at sea. Boats were normally rowed out to the fishing grounds close inshore. Si Headon's *Minnie* is on the right. (Courtesy of Stephen Perham)

Outside the Red Lion. A couple of donkeys wait for the catch to come in. Or are they waiting to carry a tourist or two up-along? (Courtesy of Stephen Perham)

Bill Braund, Fred Shackson, George Lamey and Percy Shackson inspecting a dead basking shark that had been caught in a net and hauled ashore. The biggest so caught was 26ft in length. Stephen remembers that the fishermen would often leave a tin for visitors to add a few coins to go towards the cost of a new net, although it seems that much of the money was later spent in the Red Lion! (Courtesy of Stephen Perham)

Above: Boats in the harbour again. These boats were used to take out trippers during the summer, a practice that continues today. (Mike Smylie Collection)

Left: The crew of the lifeboat in the 1880s. Robert Badcock is wearing a hat on the front row whilst the man at the back wearing a tam-o'-shanter is an inspector. The man on the back left is William Moss, the harbourmaster. (Courtesy of Stephen Perham)

having taken Rick Stein out fishing in his TV series, was built by Tom Waters and possibly owned by Jack Harris and is now on the shingle in the harbour. The other builder was J. Hinks of Appledore whose boats, according to Sidney Braund from Bucks Mills who fished from there for twenty years (aged fifty-six in 1933), were renowned for their speed, although Stephen says the Waters' boats were lighter. The Bucks Mills boats, as Braund, who in 1933 was a fishermen's agent and the Town Crier for Bideford, tells us, were 12ft carvel boats all built at Appledore by either Hinks or Thomas Williams, the latter being best for fishing and strongly built 'with a lot of bottom'. Returning to the picarooners, there is a 15ft boat hanging in the heritage centre atop the village which was most likely built by Waters in about 1938. The *Little Mary* is in the National Maritime Museum

Taking the nets ashore after the rescue of the Clovelly boat *Minnie*. The lifeboat *William Cantrell Ashley*, a Liverpool-class vessel, was the last big lifeboat in Clovelly lifeboat house. Si Headon was out fishing with the *Minnie* in October 1965 when he landed so much herring that the boat eventually sank under the weight of fish. The lifeboat rescued him and brother Norman, who couldn't swim, and salvaged the nets. It was estimated that these, when landed, held 18 mease of herring, equivalent to over 11,000 herring. (Courtesy of Stephen Perham)

John Olde with a lobster aboard his boat in the 1990s. The lobster fishery is more lucrative than herring these days. (Courtesy of Stephen Perham)

Above: A good catch. Stephen Perham, Bernard Braund, Ticker Glover and Jessica Braund clearing out the nets on the beach in the 1990s. (Courtesy of Stephen Perham)

Left: Stephen and Mark Gist clearing the nets from Stephen's picarooner. Mark was sadly drowned whilst fishing in 1998. (Courtesy of Stephen Perham)

Cornwall, Falmouth, and I met Michael whose father William owned her and whose aunt she was named after. There is a picarooner in Eyemouth that was built by Roger Hinks and another Hinks' example outside the Fire Station in Appledore with a hole in her. The other, Stephen has found and hopes to bring to Clovelly soon.

The Bucks Mills Ledge boats supposedly got their name from a submarine ledge that lies offshore, some two and a half miles east of Bucks Mills itself (or Bucksh as it's called locally). However, 'ladging' refers to fishing with lines and ground bait out on the ledge. There is also a Clovelly Ledge boat, one of which used to be in the North Devon Maritime Museum at Appledore and is about 11ft in length. In Clovelly they also went 'ladging' in the picarooners, with two men who anchor and each put down two lines. Frank Vine tells of the time he was 'ladging' close to the harbour. Whilst waiting with their lines down they cleaned up the boat, tossing a few rope ends and bits of canvas, fish bones and such overboard. Eventually they landed a big skate and in its stomach, when cut open, they found all the bits they had thrown out of the boat! Spillering was another colloquialism for long-lining.

Boyle also came across an essay that was in the possession of R. Harper of Bideford in 1946 (perhaps a relation of Charles?) and is worth a brief mention. It tells of the herring

Stephen Perham and Martel Fursdon, a first officer in the merchant navy who works aboard cruise liners and helps Stephen when she is back in Clovelly.

Mike Smylie sailing the *Little Lily* out of Clovelly Harbour in 2008. (Courtesy of Ann Cooper)

fishery which in 1929 'was exceptionally good and Appledore benefited accordingly'. The cry in Appledore by four or five cartsmen was of 'Clovelly herring, Clovelly herring', pleasant about ten o'clock in the morning. Obviously the writer was a fan of fresh herring, of which, he said, they ate three a day. The price then was sixteen for a shilling in Appledore although at Minehead they were six a penny. In Clovelly he had been informed that they were 3*s* for a long hundred (120). The writer had observed on the previous day a man in Clovelly:

> In brown canvas overalls and blue jersey cleaning out a big earthenware stein about 2ft high and 18in in diameter under the picturesque archway which stands athwart the street – the place where in Westward Ho! Kingsley places the home of Salvation Yeo's mother. The man said he was getting ready to pickle his winter herrings, which had now reached the lowest price. His stein would hold probably 250 when well packed.

He then goes on to instruct as to how the salting down process must be done as well as a bit about the natural history of the herring.

Frank Vine, mentioned above, produced a description of the congenial ambience as the herring boats returned with their catch. The boats would ground on 'The Shingle', the part of the beach between the Red Lion and Crazy Kate's Cottage:

If it was night time they'd hang two hurricane lanterns on a line between the masts and as soon as the tide was cleared alongside they'd pass the nets out and shake them, so that the herrings fell in one heap beside the boat, and the nets beside them. Then they would haul the nets into the net room in the boat again. It was a pretty sight, looking down from the lookout seat, to watch the silver fish falling out and the groups of light and figures. Then the donkeys would come...

There are also several pages of facts about the 'long-boomers' and the operation of the beam trawls. By 1900 all the trawlers (some seem to refer to them as skiffs) had winches although some of the older ones had roller windlasses. The trawl was always hauled up on the starboard side. The *Teazer* was one such trawler, 'built by old Mr Blackmore, grandfather of the present shipyard at Bideford' according to Jesse Dunn, owner and skipper of the boat. His father Bill had owned her before him and she was said to have been the smallest of the trawlers. She was built in 1884 and was 26ft in the keel, 10ft in beam and with a counter stern. Boyle obviously spent time measuring her up although unfortunately there are no lines these days remaining.

So today it is left to Stephen to continue the Clovelly tradition of herring fishing, although his brother Tom also takes part in it these days, after a long period of absence. Stephen's family have lived there for generations and he has been living and bringing up a family in Crazy Kate's Cottage upon the beach for over twenty years. Kate Lyall is said to have gone mad after watching her husband James drowning whilst out fishing out in the bay. She died demented in 1830 at the age of ninety. Stephen, after years of trying to keep traditions alive, might simply go mad as he sees the Clovelly herring as a valuable asset undervalued.

In June 2008 a new picarooner was completed by the students of the Falmouth Marine College and bought by the Clovelly Estate Company for Stephen to work. The task of construction was undertaken on the whole by four students on the course. Her shape was taken from the picarooner *Little Mary* close by, taking direct scantlings from her so that no lines plan was drawn up. The frames were cut with a little bit of refinement though the old *Little Mary* was pretty fair. Some might frown at this, deeming a set of plans vital, but the finished boat seems not to have suffered at all according to the Clovelly fishermen who are indeed happy with her. She arrived in Clovelly in that July, having been named *Little Lily* after the baby born during the year to student Mark Mitchell. The purchase by the Estate was conditional on Stephen Perham using her in his quest for the famous Clovelly herring. A hundred and fifty years or more ago there were some seventy-odd boats working from the small harbour with the quality of the fish being superb according to various reports, whilst in the 1880s it was reported that one boat could land 10,000 herring in one day, By 1900 the number of boats had abruptly declined for there were only fifteen boats – mostly picarooners – working. A century later this had been reduced further and in 2009 only Stephen and Tom bothered, even though they had some record catches. Stephen mostly uses the *Little Lily*, the boat that has appeared on television on several occasions. At the 2009 Clovelly Herring Festival it was the turn of presenter Hugh Fearnley-Whittingstall, of River Cottage fame, to have a go at emptying the nets of herring. The boat, rigged with a dipping lug main and tiny mizzen sprit, sails as easily as she is rowed, the latter being the method Stephen prefers when he is fishing just off the harbour for obvious reasons.

He fishes mostly close inshore using a drift-net of several hundred yards in length. When the tides are right, the water calm and the air dark, he fishes at night, a time the herring come to the surface to feed. Daytime fishing produces a lot less fish. Once the nets are set and attached to the bow of the picarooner, together they drift with the tide. These stay down until Stephen senses there are fish in the net and then the process of hauling begins. If the catch is meagre the fish are removed whilst at sea but if there is a bounty of herring they remain in the nets until the boat is back on shore where there are usually a few hands to help disentangle the fish. By that time Stephen's local customers would be alerted and arrive, whilst much fish is sold to market. Now that he has his own smokehouse, some might soon end up on the Devon plates as Clovelly smoked herring, one of the sweetest and daintiest herring of all.

2

THE FISHING TRADITIONS OF NORTH DEVON AND SOMERSET

In the previous chapter mention was made of the name of Hinks and Waters as being two boatbuilders working in Appledore. Tom Waters had in fact moved from Clovelly to East Bideford in about 1855 because of the railway link that connected Bideford to the national network. In 1886 the company became P.B. Waters & Sons and they were soon working from two yards in Appledore. At the same time, J. Hinks & Sons and H. Ford & Sons were two other firms of boatbuilders in Appledore. Meanwhile M.W. Blackmore had a yard in Bideford, though he also later moved to Appledore. Boatbuilding was very much alive in the town right up to the 1990s when the last yard closed, though it must be said that wooden fishing craft were not built after the 1970s. When P.B. Waters died in 1959 his son Tom continued their work for a number of years until he packed up in 1978. Subsequent to that, Fords built fibreglass vessels whilst Alan Hinks built a few historic replicas such as Drake's *Golden Hind*, a Viking longship and the seventeenth-century Hudson Bay Company's vessel *Nonsuch*, as well as a few others, until both finally closed.

Although all four firms built all sorts of vessels, including Admiralty work during the wars, it was their fishing craft that interest us here and, as we've already discussed those from Clovelly, we'll now concentrate on the salmon boats of the rivers Taw and Torridge that flow through the towns of, respectively, Barnstaple and Bideford. Generally these salmon boats were 18ft in length, clinker- then later carvel-built and had four or five thwarts for the four fishermen to row, the fifth being used to hold the net at the stern. Each builder built his boat slightly different to the other as there were no drawings.

Above: Cleaning and mending a net on the foreshore at West Appledore. The boat is one of the large 20ft boats used for all types of fishing. (Courtesy of North Devon Maritime Museum)

Left: Appledore netsmen. Left to right: Bobby Ross, John Craner, Alec Craner and John Lamey with a fair catch outside John Craner's house in Ibex Court, West Appledore, *c.*1960. (Courtesy of North Devon Maritime Museum)

These 'North Devon salmon boats', as they are known, were mostly owned by Appledore fishermen and used to fish the salmon drafts on both the Taw and the Torridge rivers. It is close to Appledore that both rivers meet before flowing out into Bideford Bay and Appledore had been a port of substance since the Middle Ages.

A draft is a fishing ground, normally a pool, within a river where it is possible to lay out a net from the riverbank by boat and bring it back to the shore. On these two rivers they were worked twice a day just before low water, through the period of slack water and into the first of the flood tide. Too much current makes the net drift away whilst the salmon would be less likely to be swimming. Both rivers had their own drafts and these stretched along the river to the town but seldom beyond, though they did, at one time, fish all the tidal part of each river. So that the licensed fishermen have an equal chance they fish each draft in rota, the order traditionally decided by taking names from a hat at the start of the fishing season in March, though they are limited to three months in the summer (June to August) nowadays.

Licences were given out to the net used for the fishery, a numbered label having to be fixed to the net as well as being painted on the sides of the salmon boat used. The nets were usually made up by the fishermen themselves – each seine-net would employ four fishers. One man, the shoreman, would stay on the bank holding the shore rope to which the end of the net was attached whilst the other three stayed in the boat. The amount of rope he paid out from the shore depended on the strength of the tide and the

Netting, Bridge Pool, Bideford, *c.*1960. (Courtesy of North Devon Maritime Museum)

Salmon-netting in Sprat Pool in the middle of the estuary using a hemp net with cork floats and lead-weighted foot rope. (Courtesy of North Devon Maritime Museum)

Rowing a draft out on the Taw near Fremington Quay. Sid Crick at the oars and John Lamey shooting the net, c.1995. The lighter nets enabled two men to work the drafts. (Courtesy of North Devon Maritime Museum)

nature of the riverbank. Two aboard the boat would then row around in a semi-circle with the third man paying out the net and then the headrope and footrope, whilst the shoreman began 'walking' the net in the same direction as the net (or tide) was going. Once they were close to the shore again, this third man would throw the pole staff (a 5ft staff attached at either end of the net that stuck into the mud) into the water and leap in to hold it. The other oarsmen would secure the boat and quickly come and help him before the net was hauled in by its head and footrope, being careful not to let any fish escape by jumping over the headrope.

Although this fishing was seasonal, and therefore part-time, it could be very profitable in the days when there were plenty of salmon. In the nineteenth century catches were good and salmon sold between 4*d* and 1*s* a pound in weight. Each crew was paid a share of the total money received from the fish dealer. A sixth went to the net, a sixth to the boat and a sixth to each crewman. Usually the 'captain' owned the boat and net, which cost at least £20 for a boat and possibly a bit more for a net and rope in the 1920s and

Stowing a net in one of the smaller boats used on the river Torridge in Bridge Pool above Bideford Long Bridge, *c*.1960. (Courtesy of North Devon Maritime Museum)

'30s. A licence at that time cost £5 but that was often advanced by the dealer who took a penny per fish for his trouble. Nets had to be preserved by being barked, ropes tarred and boats overhauled and painted. 1932 was a bonanza year in North Devon with 6,317 salmon being netted though, like all fishing, the next year could bring a dearth.

It wasn't just these drafts that captured salmon in North Devon and West Somerset. Ancient use of the various fish weirs was more deadly, and the coast between Lynmouth and Watchet was plentiful in such manmade structures. The coast was perfect: a high tidal range and shorelines made up of shingle and mud. Furthermore, natural pools and gulleys enabled the longshore fishermen – those working on or just off the shore – to build their weirs in places that meant the action of the tide wouldn't wash them away. These were constructed using a system of low stone walls built with massive stones, into which stakes were driven and a hedge woven between the stakes using hazel. The shape of these weirs was a 'V' with the pointed end away from the shoreline in the direction of the ebbing current. Between Lynmouth and Watchet, especially at those places and Porlock Weir and Minehead, the shoreline still has the remains of many of these structures. Their use dates way back and references have survived of their use here in the thirteenth century, though

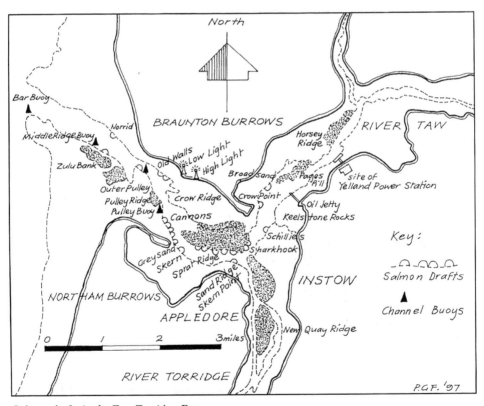

Salmon drafts in the Taw-Torridge Estuary

Sketch of salmon drafts in the estuary by Peter Ferguson.

Hauling in one of the hemp salmon nets at Old Walls on the Braunton side of the estuary. (Courtesy of North Devon Maritime Museum)

John Daniel in yellow oilskins gathering mussels during the winter months on the Taw near Yell, c.1995. The shellfish industry has now restarted after being closed for several years due to water pollution. (Courtesy of North Devon Maritime Museum)

Ilfracombe Harbour was once home to a vibrant herring fishery, though now it is mostly concerned with tourism, like many harbours around the British coast.

Watchet weir. (Mike Smylie Collection)

Right: Minehead in the late nineteenth century. The herring fishery was so prominent to the town that once the church of St Michael's used to exhibit a light from its steeple to guide the boats home. In the seventeenth and eighteenth century the harbour was crowded with smokehouses producing red and other smoked herrings. (Mike Smylie Collection)

Below: On the foreshore the remains of several fish weirs can still be seen and these were prolific catchers of fish.

Another view of one of the weirs, this being the entrance. Latterly steel poles were used instead of wooden poles, though the net entangled around the post comes from a modern trawler.

they probably existed far beyond that time. Using the natural topography of the shore to create traps was one of the first ways man caught his fish before he ventured out to sea with his hooks and nets. A few of these weirs survived into the twentieth century though by that time galvanised iron pipes were being used instead of oak stakes, and many of these still stick out of the mud.

These weirs caught all the available species of fish and were certainly not confined to catching salmon. Herring was one of the most common fish trapped and for many years large shoals of herring swam into the Bristol Channel towards the end of the year. It was not just Clovelly where herring were prolific. At Minehead, Lynmouth and Porlock Weir, smokehouses cured the herring that were caught both in weirs and by boats. Ilfracombe also had a vibrant herring fishery – and pilchards were taken there – with sixty open boats reported to be fishing locally in 1788, two years after the introduction of Government bounties to encourage such fishing.

In the rivers, especially the river Parrett, manmade basket structures called putts and putchers were set to catch salmon. Similar structures were also located around the river Severn, and around Monmouthshire, in more substantial numbers but basically they were all of the same design and much has been written about them. Basically they are conical-shaped baskets made from willow, though putts were the much larger of the two. These consisted of three separate sections – kype, butt and forewheel – which, when fixed together, meant that a putt was up to 15ft in length. The kype was the mouth with an opening 6ft in diameter whilst the smaller forewheel was where the fish became trapped

Putchers on the river Severn. These were commonplace in many of the rivers of the Bristol Channel. (Simon Cooper Collection)

Lynmouth once had a vibrant fishery and here the fishermen are standing by their boats, some of which were similar to those from Clovelly. (Mike Smylie Collection)

The remains of weirs can still be seen on the foreshore. Here the construction of the weir can clearly be seen with hazel rods weaved around the wooden posts.

as they swam in. Although extinct these days, several would be placed on the foreshore alongside each other, though during the off-season the mouth of the putt had to be closed off. Putchers, still in use in a few places on the river Severn, were much smaller baskets, some 5 or 6ft long, which were arranged in ranks, up to six putchers high and many alongside. They can be taken ashore during the closed season. It is said that before 1866 there were over 11,000 on the Severn with hundreds more on the other rivers flowing into the Bristol Channel.

Lynmouth was the centre of a large herring fishery in the sixteenth century with vast amounts being shipped up channel to Bristol. This fishery lasted from Michaelmas to Christmas and fishermen from all around the Bristol Channel were attracted to Lynmouth and many of these people rented cottages for the three-month period. Minehead had its own herring fishery at the same time and the quayside was said to be a bustle of smokehouses. Red herring – herring heavily salted and smoked for a considerable time after which time they turn red – were popular though kippers were also smoked. Four thousand barrels were exported from this, one of the smallest herring ports in Britain. It is said hostels opened up to cater for the fish buyers who flocked to the town. Ilfracombe and Lynmouth were also renowned for their red herrings which were exported far and wide. 'Combe smoked herring was deemed a delicacy in parts of Europe. Even Barnstaple had its herring salting and smoking houses on the Strand where herring sold at sixty per shilling at the end of the nineteenth century.

Above: A weir under the shadow of the first Severn Bridge, on the English side of the river.

Right: Another view of the same weir showing the remains of the posts in the mud.

The remains of a weir at Porlock Weir, although the name of the place comes from the type of harbour and not the fish weir.

Porlock Weir is a prime example of a weir harbour where the harbour has been built around a natural pool behind a shingle bank, into which the tide flooded and ebbed each day. This type of harbour, fed by streams coming down from nearby hills, is one of Britain's earliest harbour types and Porlock is a rare and unique survivor from an age before the growth of major ports. There were others along this coast, of course, such as at Minehead and Dunster, the former being allowed to decay before today's harbour wall was built as a protection for vessels, whilst Dunster's disappeared from lack of use. Porlock's natural harbour was built up and expanded around the fifteenth century so that quays and other facilities for shipping were created which in turn encouraged trade and larger trading vessels. This coast, up to the end of the nineteenth century, was simply bustling with maritime activity. Each port developed in its own particular way with fishing, importing and exporting agricultural and domestic goods, industrial trading and any other maritime activity taking precedent.

Porlock also had an oyster fishery. In a similar way to that of parts of South Wales (as we shall see in a subsequent chapter), offshore oyster beds were dredged by Porlock-based boats. These vessels, about 25ft in length, numbered no more than about a dozen at any one time during the second half of the nineteenth century. The half-decked craft were deep hulled with a pronounced sheer and were said to resemble the Bristol Channel pilot cutters. Once dredged, the oysters were brought ashore and kept in the old fish weirs until they were sent to market. With the arrival of the railway at Minehead

Porlock Weir in 1907 with the last surviving oyster dredger, the sloop-rigged *Laureate*, which continued working up to about 1915 when the oyster fishery disappeared. (Mike Smylie Collection)

in 1874, the oysters could be whisked off by train and arrive in the London restaurants the very same day.

The last oyster vessel to survive was the *Laureate* which, in 1914, was refitted with funding from the Government in a half-hearted attempt to re-establish this oyster fishery. Two years earlier, when the harbour was popular with pleasure yachtsmen from across the Channel, the derelict vessels were cleared out and the entrance dredged. At this time the remains of some twelve old oyster vessels were finally disposed of. Only the *Laureate* survived, though it is not known where she finally ended her days. In the same way, the builders of these craft are uncertain though it is known that various boatbuilders worked near to the harbour. The Pollard brothers were primarily herring fishermen and boat repairers though they did build several craft. Other builders of vessels worked up to the end of the nineteenth century, utilising local oak, elm and larch.

3

BRIDGWATER BAY AND THE LAST OF THE MUD-HORSE FISHERS

It's a blustery day in June as I park up atop the shingle bank of the flood defence at Stolford, a tiny hamlet overlooking the western end of Bridgwater Bay, and await the ebbing tide. I'd just met Brendan Sellick in his small fish hut just along the road and, once the tide had begun to uncover the vast expanse of mudflats, Brendan's son Adrian was going to take me out to his nets that lay somewhere out below the waves which were being kicked up by the brisk north-easterly wind.

Adrian arrived some time later in his four-wheel-drive jeep and in I got before we trundled off, down onto the foreshore to bump and jolt along, over the boulders and stones, the track visible ahead from many years of being driven over. Then it was along a shallow stream that wound its way amongst the rocks, the muddy water probably almost 2ft deep. The geology was astonishing: parallel lines of clusters of broken rock shelves angled at forty-five degrees running several hundred yards, like soldiers on parade. We passed through gaps where the rock had been cut away, presumably by the action of the running water. Beyond the rocks were fields of glistening mud. After fifteen minutes or so Adrian turned the vehicle around to face onshore and out we got into the world of mud. Close by was one of his mud-horses; a wooden structure some 6ft long and 3ft wide with elm boards curving up at the front to form a wide skid, and which was weighted down with a number of large stones to prevent the tide washing it away. This was the vehicle to transport fish across the vast mud flats and it looked almost prehistoric with its worn timbers and mud encrustation, though Adrian told me it was only three years old. He

An old photo entitled 'Sellicks Rook' with Brendan Sellick, his son Adrian and fellow fisherman, one of the family cousins, in 1970. (Courtesy of Brendan Sellick)

then instructed me to walk along one of the seaweed-covered stony banks, across some mud and to follow the line of stakes to where his nets were, visible as they were several hundred yards further out. He began to lift off the stones to free the mud-horse before pushing it the direct route to the nets.

After a good trudge through mud that flowed over the tops of my wellies and which almost succeeded in getting me to fall over when attempting to take a photograph, I arrived on the solid ground where the nets were. These were strung to a series of posts perpendicular to the shoreline and held up by posts driven into the mud which were some 6ft high. I should have followed Adrian's example, I thought, as I sloshed around with boots full of water, for he was wearing shorts and trainers, though he admitted that he didn't always.

An old photograph of the stake nets in Bridgwater Bay. (Courtesy of John Nash)

One of the mud-horse fishermen back in the 1950s. (Courtesy of John Nash)

Brendan Sellick pushing his mud-horse in the 1980s. (Courtesy of John Nash)

Three gutted skate hanging on the gate by the fish shop.

How to get service in the shop!

Adrian Sellick preparing to empty and set his nets.

'I persevere as long as I can in shorts but in winter it gets too cold.'

'You mean you come out here in winter?' I replied in surprise.

'All year round when the tides are right. Maybe on the neaps I have a few days off. Sometimes the weather is too bad, but, yes, most days I'm here. It used to be me and father but now it's just me.'

We inspect the nets. Firstly there are a line of twenty-eight shrimp nets; nets with a square mouth several feet across and which are funnel-shaped to decrease to the cod-end some 6ft downstream. Each is untied, the contents emptied into a sieve before the net is carefully tied up again. The catch is sorted – the small fish, weed and bits of rubbish are extracted – after which it is added to the slowly filling basket. This catch consists of shrimps, dabs, Dover sole, whiting, the odd mullet, dogfish and skate. The latter was expertly sliced to separate the edible wings. You can certainly tell an experienced fisherman by the way he cuts a skate. Then he cleared the few stake nets which held the odd fish before we trudged another few hundred yards through mud and water out to a further line of stake nets set out by the low water mark. Here were two more skate, mullet, dogfish and a couple of decent-sized Dover soles.

'Do you come out here every time?' I asked.

'Normally but there wasn't much yesterday so I thought that I might hang them up today if there was nothing. It saves the tide ripping them. This wind brings a lot of weed down off the beaches too. But there's not much time out here. By the time we get back to the jeep this lot will be under water.'

Fish in the nets.

Emptying the nets.

Into a riddle to remove the unwanted stones, seaweed, small fish and so on.

Leaving behind a few small fish and shrimps.

'Have you ever been caught out?'

'Once. Then you have to walk right round there.' He pointed to a line of stakes further upstream on what looked like solid rock. 'It's much further but I put those stakes there just in case.'

As we sloshed our way back, my boots still full, the dangers out here were obvious. It wasn't a place to mess about, especially when the mud was many feet deep in places. Once we arrived back at the mud-horse, Adrian loaded up his baskets and, whilst I retraced my steps through the stream and mud, he pushed his contraption straight across the mud back to the jeep. By leaning upon the framework, he can push it forward without his feet sinking too far into the mud. However, it did look hard work.

'Not half as hard as carrying the fish in a basket though,' said Adrian when I mentioned that. He had a point.

'Years ago we had to push it right to the foreshore. There was no driving the jeep down here,' he told me as he unloaded the baskets and weighted down the mud-horse with the large boulders again. 'It was all mud, no rock. Until they built the power station there. Changed the nature of the beach then, they did, and almost destroyed the fishing too. They suck in more fish than I can dream of in one day. They have a filter in their cooling-water intake and they used to put the fish in a skip round the back. Stank, it did, at times. Now they don't but they seem to hide it.'

The power station in question was the Hinckley Point nuclear power station of which there were two, though one has since been decommissioned. It seems a French company

Before the end of the net is re-tied.

The seagulls fight for the discards.

Emptying another net – note how the ends are fixed.

Above: More screaming gulls, though they are the only other creatures out here.

Right: The skate are gutted immediately.

Adrian prepares to wade through the mud to his stake nets at the low water mark. Time is of the essence if he is not to get marooned out here.

An unlucky mullet in the net.

Gutting another skate. Skate are fairly common in these nets.

had been buying up the land around the site in preparation to build either one or two more stations, given the political will to concentrate more of Britain's power generating from this source. Police patrols had become almost constant, a sinister development, especially given the formation of a dedicated squad of armed police for this sole purpose.

We soon arrived back at Brendan's fish hut where he was preparing to process the catch. Adrian went off for a deserved shower whilst I was determined to ask Brendan more about the traditions of this fishery which I presumed was an age-old method.

'Well, I started when I was fourteen, when I was a kid. My dad was here all his life and I carried on from him. I've done it for sixty-odd years, my dad did it the same, his father did it the same and the grandfather before him started it in 1820 or something. He was a stonemason, he picked up with a local fisher-girl and she persuaded him there was money in fishing and that's how we came here. Of course there were a lot of families doing it in those days. Any amount. When I started there were three or four families, a dozen blokes, nine brothers and that. Fifteen years ago there were two families. All had their own patch and a licence. That's only a few quid today but it gives us reassurance.'

He paused for a few seconds before continuing.

'Yes, non-stop for sixty-odd years, I can't believe it. Adrian went out when he was six or so. Some blokes from Burnham did it using a boat to get out to their nets. I remember one father and son one Sunday whilst we were out. They disappeared whilst out trammelling in their punt. Went in they did and weren't found for three weeks.

Probably one got caught in the net when it went over and the other went in to save him. Lost their knife they must have. Yes, many have lost their lives out here where all sorts of things can happen.'

I'd heard that there were mud-fishermen over on the Welsh coast so I asked him about it.

'Back in the early 1800s there were too many here so a couple of them moved over there; Cardiff Bay. One of them had a shop in Splott and he did the market and also had a barrow. Then my uncle George Sellick did it over in Cardiff. They went from here to Cardiff, his father did it. It finished up in 1939 at the outbreak of war. Bombing times. We were stopped for fishing for one year during the war. One year. That's all.'

A family of customers arrived to buy fish. Eventually they decided on a dozen dabs – dabbies they called them – which cost £7.50 which seemed very reasonable. Two skate wings had cost an earlier customer £4.

'People phone up. That's how we want it. Some of the time we had to stop people as we had nothing. So they phone and ask what time to come. Most of them do.'

I asked what the catch generally is. Was today's typical?

'Shrimps are coming in now. These are a bit small but they'll start coming now and once they start coming they'll come thick and get bigger. Brown shrimps. Skate, Dover sole, whiting, bass in the summer. The very occasional salmon. No bass today but some days there's half a dozen. A lot of mullet, flounders, dabs. Doggies I skin and sell for £1.50. We used to go all over the place. Bristol, Cardiff, Weston, London even. Took it to Bridgwater to put on the train. Twenty years ago or more. Went there by horse and cart at one time. Then I used to drive over to Weston twice a week to deliver to about twelve

Adrian pushing the mud-horse.

Building the stones up around the mud-horse to prevent it being washed away by the strong tides.

fish shops. None there now, I think. One in Burnham maybe. Lloyds the fish merchants in Whiteladies Road in Bristol. He used to ring up and he'd be here in an hour. Different people would come and pick it up. Couple of hotels ring up and take a few mullet or a bass. Old folk used to come and buy shrimps to sell around the pubs. It used to supplement their pension. They can't do that now. In autumn, that's the best time. A lot of skate, cod, whiting and coming into winter sprats and whitebait. Little baby whitebait. Cod, cod and more cod in winter. Bass very early this year, earlier than anywhere else. Think they come up channel to spawn. Yes, it was quite an industry years ago. We had seventy or a hundred shrimp nets and much more gill netting. Now we are the last and just manage to survive.'

Adrian had already told me that he couldn't have more nets because he wouldn't have enough time to empty them. Two hours out on the mud is a maximum and sometimes it's less. When the two of them fished they could service more nets but now that he's alone he can't and his sons aren't keen to carry on. To take on someone else would mean having to pay out wages which the business wouldn't support. Brendan continued:

'I make the nets in winter as well. I made a lot this winter. Hell of a lot. Twenty over the last couple of months. You can't do them in five minutes as there's quite a bit of work in them, shrimp nets. They have to be done properly or they wouldn't last five minutes. If you had to buy them they'd charge quite a lot of money. It takes several hours to make one of them.'

Brendan had lit the shrimp boiler in preparation to boil the shrimps that he had been washing whilst chatting.

As soon as Adrian arrives back with the catch he's off for a shower. Brendan has to clean the catch ready to sell. Boiling up the shrimps in the boiler is another of his jobs.

'These little shrimps are very popular. Brown shrimps. In a month's time when they get a bit bigger and the quality's a bit better, they sell very well. Yes, very well. We get a few pink shrimps when the wind goes to the west and blows them out of the rocks. And a few prawns. But 90 per cent is brown shrimp. See the white shrimp there. A sort of albino shrimp. We call them whiteshanks. You can eat them. Seems they are peculiar to the Bristol Channel and they used to catch a lot of them down at Watchet.'

The first batch of shrimps went into the boiler where they stayed for a few minutes before Brendan tipped them into a large round shallow basket which he called a 'reap'. They used to have two dozen reaps full of shrimps, whilst today he'd be lucky to fill half of one. We talked about the loss of mud which he put down to the actual structure of the power station which, he thought, caused eddies in the prevailing wind which moved the stream. The mud has undoubtedly gone down several feet in depth and, as both Sellicks pointed out, Mother Nature usually takes generations to make such drastic changes but they had only noticed the mud removal since the power station was built. However, as is always the case, the lack of precise data means that British Energy or anyone attached to them simply deny the facts. To them it's either a natural phenomenon or simply a coincidence. Then the talk moved onto supermarkets, as it generally does, and how fish shops had since disappeared. Why, I wondered, is it always the large conglomerates that destroy the livelihoods of those following the traditional ways that had otherwise survived generations before these wieldy conglomerates came along? By the time we'd finished Brendan had boiled the entire catch, which didn't amount to much more than 15lb. Then, just as I was leaving, he showed me the eel tank outside, alongside the shed. Eel catches, though, were poor again, largely because a ton of elvers had been caught from the river Parrett which had been shipped straight to Japan. Not surprising, the eel population had shrunk drastically.

As I left I wondered what will happen when Adrian packs up. Are grants available? As Brendan says: 'They give a man thirty-thousand a year and a new Land Rover just to count the birds or to see how many mushrooms are going down the field and to record everything. So why not to keep the mud-horse going?' Exactly. Why not provide some assistance to keep these traditions going. As he spoke I suddenly pictured the film crew that Adrian told me he once took out. I could see them with their gear trudging through the mud. They were Americans he said. I think of the film people I'd come across with their pretences and arrogance and somehow couldn't see them plodding out to film Adrian at work. Thankfully these did but in time their footage might be the only evidence that mud-horse fishing ever existed. Luckily Adrian, he told me, loves it out on the mud, the day-dreaming and peace away from the pressure of society. True, he has another job working nights in the local yogurt factory and I have to wonder how and when he sleeps sometimes. But to both him and Brendan they have something worth hanging on to, in their eyes; something unique in British waters and something that not only brings in an income, however small, but remains a tangible link to their family's past. One can only hope that this does not become yet another tradition faded into the memory of the few that care.

4

THE SOMERSET FLATNERS – WORKBOATS OF A VANISHED PURPOSE

According to Tony James, Combwich, on the left bank of the river Parrett, was once the stronghold of the flatner, the flat-bottomed boat of Somerset. Today that stronghold has moved along the coast to Watchet where, in the Watchet Boat Museum, there is the largest collection in the world. Or so the leaflet of the museum says. We needed to visit to make sure!

It's easy to find as it's housed in the Old Brunel Railway Goods Shed alongside the steam railway close to the entrance of Watchet. It's free to enter – check opening hours – and inside there are several flatners of different sizes and vintage. The oldest currently is from the early part of the twentieth century, whilst two new boats are also on show. Fishing equipment abounds, as do old photographs and various other exhibits relevant to the flatners, their use or merely Watchet itself. The shed simply oozes flatner culture as would be expected but is as much about the folk who sailed and rowed the boats as it is of the boats themselves. Well worth the visit indeed.

To say that a flatner was primarily a fishing boat would be incorrect. It was, as were many boats of a similar size and construction, the workhorse of riverbank-dwellers and workers. Thus they carried withies and turf around the Somerset Levels, reeds from where they had been cut, coal from South Wales, animals to market and trippers out to sea. Fishing, nonetheless, probably had the greatest influence upon them in their development. Whereas the 16ft-long so-called *withy boats* and *turf boats* were small and crudely built with a single 1in-thick oak bottom simply to work on the shallow waterways of the

Some of the boats and displays inside the Watchet Boat Museum.

Ex-RN Lt-Col Billington and his wife show their home, Turkey Cottage near Bridgwater, well flooded. He borrowed the boat which was built using withy boat lines from Eric McKee's book *Working Boats of Britain*. Boat no longer exists but Billington has since built a tank around the cottage. (Courtesy of John Nash)

A postcard postmarked 1905 showing a flatner off Burnham. (Courtesy of John Nash)

Workers of the
Somerset River
Board using two of
their boats to form a
bridge to cross with
their wheelbarrows.
(Courtesy of John
Nash)

Stake nets put up
at Black Rock by
fisherman Bob Thorne
at the end of the salmon
butt season. (Courtesy
of John Nash)

Bob Thorne's hut at
Black Rock with his
two boats. (Courtesy of
John Nash)

No. of Issue   195

THE SALMON AND FRESHWATER FISHERIES ACT 1923.

Fishery District of the Rivers Avon, Brue and Parret.

LICENCE TO FISH.

𝕎E, the Board of Conservators appointed for the Fishery District of the Rivers Avon, Brue, and Parret, and their Tributaries, the area comprising (1) such parts of the administrative counties of Gloucester, Somerset, Wilts, Dorset, Devon, and the county boroughs of Bath and Bristol as lie within the natural watershed of any river or stream which flows into the sea between the following points, namely :—(a) The seaward extremity at high-water mark of the right or eastern bank of the stream flowing into the sea in the Parish of Oare in the County of Somerset at or near the boundary between the counties of Devon and Somerset ; and (b) The site of the Avon Battery in the County of Gloucester ; (2) the space between ordinary high and low-water mark (hereinafter termed the foreshore) between the said points ; and (3) the sea adjoining to the foreshore between the said points for the distance of three miles seaward from ordinary low-water mark, but excluding any portion of the Usk and Severn Fishery Districts as laid down on the map deposited in the Office of the Clerk to the Board of Conservators at 13, Castle Street, Bridgwater, in the County of Somerset, by virtue of the powers vested in us under the Salmon and Freshwater Fisheries Act, do hereby authorise and empower *Cecil John Reasons.*

of *Myrtle Cottage Pawlett*

in the County of Somerset, to fish with *Dip Net.*

for Salmon within the said District, in which he is otherwise so entitled to fish by law he having paid

the sum of *Ten shillings* for this Licence, to Mr. ~~A. J. Whitby~~ *L. E. Phillips*, residing at Bridgwater,

in the County of Somerset, who is hereby authorised to receive the same on behalf of us the Board

of Conservators.

This Licence will expire on the 31st day of August, 19

Given under the Seal of the said Board this *15th*

day of *May*   19 *33*   *L. E. Phillips*

3·30 p. m.

This Licence is only available within the District in respect of the instrument named for the use of the person to whom it is issued.
    Any person using any kind of instrument (except Rod and Line) for catching Salmon without a proper Licence, is liable to a penalty of £20.
    A Licensee, on producing his Licence, may require any person found Fishing for Salmon in any manner to produce his Licence ; and he is also bound to produce his Licence on demand made by any Licensee, Conservator, or Water Bailiff, under a penalty of £5 for refusal.
    The open season for Fishing with Nets and any other kind of instrument (except Rod and Line) is from 6 o'clock on Monday morning to 6 o'clock on Saturday mornings, in every week, and extends from 2nd February to 31st August inclusive.   Penalty for Fishing during the Annual or Weekly Close Time, £5 besides forfeiture of Fish, and £2 additional for each Fish caught.
    All unseasonable Fish, and the young of Salmon, commonly known (among other names) as Samlet, Smolt, Par, and Lastspring, taken accidentally, must be forthwith returned to the water with the least possible injury or the taker will render himself liable to the penalties of the Act.
    Every person (notwithstanding he is Licensed to Fish) is liable to the penalties imposed by the Salmon and Freshwater Fisheries Act, and a Licensee for a second offence forfeits his Licence.

Cecil John Reasons' licence to fish for 1933. Cecil was Bob Thorne's mentor according to John Nash of the Watchet Boat Museum.

Levels where they were pulled along, the fishing boats worked in more of a constraining environment. The river Parrett has been described as one of Britain's most dangerous rivers because of its high spring tidal range, which brings its strong currents, and the fact that it is immensely muddy with all the silt it carries down. In the nineteenth century over a hundred people drowned in it and many vessels were caught out and subsequently sunk in its grip. Thus the *river boats* were a bit longer than the upstream craft – always about 19ft and 5ft 6in in beam – and they fished under oars upon the river mainly for salmon, using a dip-net, or to spear eels. The oars favoured were unusual in that they had

SOMERSET RIVER BOARD

Nº 27

RIVER BOARDS ACT, 1948.

SALMON & FRESHWATER FISHERIES ACTS, 1923 & 1935

LICENCE TO FISH FOR SALMON

Mr. R. Thorne of *Myrtle Cottage, Stretchill*

in the County of *Somerset* having paid the sum of *10* s. *-* d.

for this Licence is hereby authorised to fish for Salmon with *a dip net* in any waters in which he is

otherwise entitled so to fish within the area of the Somerset River Board.

This Licence will expire on the 31st day of August, 19 *52*

Dated this *19* day of *April* 19 *52*

pp. ....

Clerk of the Board.

The Annual Close Season for salmon fishing is the period from 31st August to the 1st February following and the weekly close time (Except for rod and line or putts and putchers) is the period between 6 o'clock a.m., on Saturday and 6 o'clock a.m., on Monday.

The Licensee fishing in pursuance of this Licence is bound under a penalty, to produce it when called upon (1) by any Licensee under the Salmon and Freshwater Fisheries Acts, 1923 and 1935, who produces his licence, and to furnish his name and address (2) by any member or officer of the Somerset River Board who produces a Certificate of his being a member or officer signed by the Clerk of the River Board (3) by any Water Bailiff appointed under the said Acts who produces the instrument appointing him (4) by any Constable.

This licence does not give permission to the Holder to fish any water unless the prior consent of the person or persons possessing the fishing rights has been obtained.

Any person using any kind of instrument for catching Salmon without a proper Licence is liable to a penalty.

Bob Thorne's licence for 1952.

Eddie and Cecil Reasons dipping for salmon on the river Parrett, in the 1980s. (Courtesy of John Nash)

Above: Eddie Reasons with his dip net. (Courtesy of John Nash)

Left: Bill Pococke with the net he used to catch fish with from the bank of the Parrett in Bridgwater, hence the street's name 'Salmon Parade'. (Courtesy of John Nash)

A photo of a butt, taken
by Dr Dennis Chapman
in the 1960s. (Courtesy of
Dennis Chapman)

square shafts instead of the more normal round ones. Each boat always carried a wooden bailer. The salmon were said to swim upriver and when their gills became choked with the mud when up close to Bridgwater itself they surfaced because they couldn't swim for more than 25 yards without clearing. The fisherman rowed to where the fish is seen to clear and then dipped his net where he expected him to surface again. For the patient fisherman the rewards could be good but although it sounds easy, it was said to be very hard work. There were once some twenty licences issued to permit fishing in the river, though catches declined after the 1930s, due partly to pollution. Further downriver, the *sea boats* were of a similar size but fitted with a small sprit sail and jib, a long rudder and a centreboard for sailing efficiency. These were the boats that were said to have sailed over to South Wales to collect coal and even sheep at times.

Just to confuse, some *sea boats* were also known as *gore boats* or *bay boats*, the former being used to service the stake nets out on the Gore Bank of Bridgwater Bay whilst the *bay boats*, as the name suggests, worked further out into the same bay, fishing for sprats,

Left: Bob Thorne making a butt. (Courtesy of John Nash)

Below: Cecil Reasons with a good sea trout, *c.*1960. (Courtesy of John Nash)

herring, mackerel and shrimps. What they all had in common was a similar construction. Based on a flat bottom, though the more seaworthy boats had a slight rockering to this, they had no keel and steeply raking stem and stern posts. The sides were traditionally built up from three planks of elm – either in a flat, carvel or clinker construction way, the latter where each plank overlapped the other. The bottom consisted of five oak planks laid side by side. Strengthening to the hull was provided by internal framing in oak. A finished flatner of about 19ft weighed almost a ton, so heavily built were the boats used out in the bay.

A specimen butt and a flatner obviously posed for the camera. (Courtesy of John Nash)

A postcard view of Watchet in the 1950s. (Courtesy of John Nash)

Boatbuilder Harold Kimber with the flatner which he restored and which is now in the museum. (Courtesy of John Nash)

Launch day of *Yankee Jack* in Watchet Harbour, July 1997. (Courtesy of John Nash)

John Short, otherwise known as
Yankee Jack, who died in 1933.
(Courtesy of John Nash)

One unique way of fishing was once practised on the lower reaches of the river Parrett. Although similar to two methods we will learn about in subsequent chapters – stop-netting and compass-netting – here they called it 'pitching' and it seems to have been equally hazardous. In this case the fishermen would moor two boats alongside each other off the rocks with anchors bow and stern so that the boats lay across the stream. The net was fixed to a V-shaped affair, about 20ft across the mouth on 15ft poles. This was lowered into the water so that the bag of the net trailed beneath both boats and it was held down by the fisherman who stood in the second boat, even though the net was balanced against the gunwale of the first boat. Fisherman Bob Thorpe, well known in the area, described the way he fished: 'Plenty of bosom, see, and the bosom used to go straight back under the boat. Well then you 'ad your finger in the mesh, see, and soon's you felt a tug you knew something 'ad gone in the net.'

As to the danger of this method, Bob again: 'When you did weight your net down, generally two of 'ee there see, and one, like the one, er, 'ad a axe in 'is 'and so that if anythink went wrong, you know like the boat started to tip or anything, and you couldn't release the net, 'e'd just chop the anchor line and the boat would swing round, bow on to the tide, see.'

Putchers were used on the river Parrett as well, as were butts which is what they call 'putts' around here. They've been described in a previous chapter.

A sculpture of Yankee Jack looks out over Watchet Harbour which is now a marina.

A Weston-super-Mare flatner sailing off the town. (Courtesy of John Nash)

In Watchet, where maritime matters were important back in Celtic times, their flatners were called *flatties*. They differed to the others only in the fact that they had an extra layer of planking on the bottom because of the nature of the rocky foreshore over which they were launched. Watchet has had a harbour for at least 500 years, probably much longer as it known that the Scandinavians raided the town in the tenth century. Thus it is possible that the same Norse men – either Vikings or Danes – found the locals fishing in their small flat-bottomed craft. Such craft can be found all over Europe, even today, and the fact that Caesar saw similar craft in north-west France centuries before makes this a distinct possibility. It has been said that the Newfoundland dories – the small boats that accompany the large cod-fishing ships – bear a strong resemblance to flatners and that their influence may have come from flatners that were carried over by Somerset ships in the days they sailed across the Atlantic in search of cod. Indeed, further suggestions that they may be related to the medieval cogs – the flat-bottomed trading vessels of the Southern North Sea – are again not impossible. Similar flat-bottomed craft – called cots – can be seen today across St George's Channel in south-east Ireland, where they still work the river Slaney that emerges into the sea at Wexford. Strangely, there's a deeper water version of the cot that works around Wexford Harbour and out to sea and is very different to the river cot. This again bears a distinct resemblance to the flatners of Weston-super-Mare which, apart from sharing the same name and also having a flat bottom, have no other characteristics of the Watchet flatties.

Motorised Weston flatners taking trippers out. (Courtesy of John Nash)

Basil Greenhill and his wife in their dory, which some say evolved from the flatner. (Courtesy of John Nash)

A Bridgwater barge being used to take trippers on an outing on the river Tone. Bridgwater was once an important coastal trading port. These flat-bottomed dumb barges, limited to 52ft in length due to lock dimensions, worked the rivers upstream of the town, carrying coal, agricultural goods, fish, withies and building materials. They were propelled by the two crew members, one using a sweep set into a groove in the top of the sternpost and another in a moveable oarlock forward. They carried up to 25 tons of cargo at a time. (Courtesy of John Nash)

For almost one hundred years the flattie disappeared from the day-to-day workings of Watchet Harbour until the first replica was built in the late 1990s. Constructed of a red pine bottom with plywood sides and laminated frames to reduce the overall weight of the boat, the boat was modelled on one of only a few flatties known to have survived. Although the original builder was unknown, it had been used in the river Parrett and around Bridgwater Bay before being restored in the 1960s by local renowned boatbuilder Harold Kimber who worked in Highbridge. The replica flattie – called *Yankee Jack* after Watchet-born seaman and shanty-man John Short, otherwise known as Yankee Jack – was launched in 1997 and in 2002 was sailed by her owner Tony James around the south-west coast which resulted in his book *Yankee Jack Sails Again*. She is now one of the new boats resting in the museum.

The Weston-super-Mare flatners – not flatties, mind – were more of an offshore boat. Weston was a flourishing fishing village back before the Victorians transformed it into an equally flourishing seaside resort with its well-known pier. The fishermen's boats were about the same length in general – around 20ft – though it is said a few were built towards the 30ft mark. They were transom-sterned unlike the double-ended Parrett flatners and Watchet flatties (we mention both here to avoid confusion, though they were the same thing!) and were good sailing craft. Rigged with one sprit sail normally, they ran out to Flat Holm and Steep Holm fishing for sprats and herring, and sometimes shrimps,

Barges lying alongside at Bridgwater, whilst one coastal vessel can be seen downstream of the bridge. Many barges carried coal to the Bath brick kilns upstream and returned with a cargo of the bricks. In between they collected the slimy mud used as the raw material for the bricks. These were then exported as far as the Mediterranean and North Africa. Some barges were used for salmon fishing as well. (Courtesy of John Nash)

salmon and haddock during the summer season. The small Steep Holm was where a group of Viking/Danish raiders were driven after an unsuccessful raid upon Watchet in 914 though they came back again. In 1776 a refuge hut was built there for the use and safety of any fisherman having the misfortune of finding himself there.

As tourism developed in Weston – and nearby Clevedon – the flatners grew a little in size and some had two masts to accommodate trippers who took the chance for a short voyage around the locality. By about 1900 there were still about ten flatners working, unlike at Watchet. A few were later fitted with inboard engines, though these were only used for pleasure. Weston's fishing traditions were well out the door. Only a couple of Weston flatners exist today, one of which, *Flare*, being in the Weston Museum. She was built with a motor and never had sails. The 1936-built *Ann* is currently under restoration. But things do come back, and as Weston's grand pier is opened once again after its disastrous fire, hopefully *Ann* will take to the water again and maybe someone will then build another replica Weston flatner so that the two can sail against each other. I'm not holding my breath though!

5

AROUND BRISTOL'S FLOATING HARBOUR

Bristol was never much of a fishing port even if it did have its designated fishing registration letters of BL. Very few vessels were ever registered there though the fact that some were suggests a local ownership rather than working local waters. Some BL-registered vessels worked out of Milford Haven and Cardiff. Before the railways changed the face of Britain in the first half of the nineteenth century some fish was landed directly into Bristol though the few miles up the river Avon to the port itself must have been an inconvenience. Once fish could be loaded onto a train from Swansea or Cardiff and rushed along to Bristol, no sane fisher was going to bother plodding upriver. What today Bristol does have, however, is a strong maritime tradition kept alive by the owners of historic craft, most of whom are enthusiast individuals.

It is probable that most people today do not associate the Bristol Channel as a place to charter a boat. The strong tides, high tidal height, fierce south-west winds lay bear to the Channel and the generally poor British weather all add up to persuade people to go elsewhere, preferably to warmer climes or, if the weather and midges don't thwart you, to Western Scotland. Another nearer option is the south coast, with its easily accessible sailing grounds of Cornwall, Scilly and France. Wherever you choose, you are likely to come across the odd Bristol-built boat.

Walk along the harbour in 2011 and you might be forgiven in thinking that several fishing boats did in fact work from Bristol for there are several dotted around, moored amongst the barges, yachts and larger vessels. A few, based on the Scottish Motor Fishing Vessel (MFV) design, are more houseboats than sea boats, whose owners forgo the

Bristol did have a fishing fleet. Here the steam fishing boat BL10, BL representing Bristol, is pictured alongside the fish market in Milford Haven around 1900. (Mike Smylie Collection)

The 1925-built *Tangaroa* sailing in the Bristol Harbour Festival in August 2010.

The *Tangaroa* passing Cabot's Tower. She is today used as a charter boat out of Bristol Docks, one of a few boats to operate in such a way.

Another Danish-built boat is *Vilma*, here for the Harbour Festival in 2010. She was restored as a Welsh topsail schooner by Bangor-based boatbuilder Scott Metcalfe.

The *Matthew* and the Scottish fishing boat *Courageous* at the Harbour Festival in 2006.

hassle of living ashore for life afloat, even if the shore only remains a couple of feet away. However, there are others that offer a very different view of life.

Tangaroa is one such vessel. Built as *Tina* by Søren Larsen of Nykøbing Mors, Denmark in 1925, she fished the North Sea until moving to Britain in the 1970s. For the last few years she has been owned and based in Bristol Docks from where she runs charter trips throughout the Bristol Channel and as far away as Brittany. Danish vessels such as she is, often called *kotters*, worked under sail until engines were fitted in the 1930s. When these vessels came to be retired from fishing there were literally hundreds of them for sale in the various Danish fishing ports such as Esbjerg. Another *kotter*, the 1931-built *Josefine*, was launched as the *Lilly*, L60 from the Andersen & Ferdinandsen yard at Gilleleje, Denmark and nowadays charters out of nearby Watchet. The third of these erstwhile Danish craft is the *Leason*, built as the *Corona* at the Jensen & Lauridsen Shipyard in Esbjerg in 1931 for S. Christensen and registered as E468. The boat stayed in his family for twenty-five years before being sold in 1956 and by 1970 she was owned by E.S. Pedersen and had been renamed *Bente Stenberg*, E468. By 1977 she had been bought by Vagn Pedersen (possibly a relative) and renamed again as *Minna*, E468. Three years later she was under British ownership, working as *Leason*, GY440, out of Grimsby. Then in the mid-1980s she was bought at scrap value by Dave Blackham and she arrived in Bristol, stripped of her fishing gear, and he started converting her into a pleasure boat. However, she was sold

A converted Watson lifeboat on the left, a multi-coloured ex-Danish fishing boat and, against the barge on the extreme right, painted pale blue, is the Bristol pilot boat *Peggy*.

A view of Pill in the late nineteenth century when Pill was the base of the Bristol pilots. (Mike Smylie Collection)

Above: A raft of over a dozen pilot boats moored at Pill at the end of the nineteenth century. (Mike Smylie Collection)

Left: The pilot boat *Petrel* at Pill about 1900. (Mike Smylie Collection)

Hand-over day of *Mischief* at the Underfall Yard in Bristol in November 2007.

again in the 1990s and, under the proposal of being converted for offshore charter work, she was taken to Tommi Nielsen's boatyard in Gloucester Docks. With no money being handed over, she soon sank and I guess it was luck that she wasn't chainsawed up as many of these craft were. Instead she was towed down to Sharpness and thence to Portishead, where I first saw her languishing on the quay in a very sorry state. A few months later I returned to Portishead to photograph her and she'd gone. It wasn't for several months that I found out why. Just before the bulldozers were to set upon her because she was

John Raymond-Barker alongside the boat he built on spec and sold before completion.

Side view of the pilot boat *Pegasus*, built by Bristol boatbuilder Mark Rolt under the name of Bristol Classic Boats.

sitting where more waterside housing was to be built, she was purchased and moved to Bristol by boatbuilder Ben Punter and his partner Phoebe, where she is now at the Underfall Yard afloat and under restoration. She joins the growing bands of *kotters* to be restored, becoming yet another of these lovely curved, graceful yet tough masters of the North Sea given a new lease of life.

Though not Danish-built, another ex-fishing boat from the sail era is the Thames bawley *Fiddle*, recently arrived from Cornwall. The Scottish ex-fishing vessel *Courageous*, fitted out as a pleasure craft, was built as a ring-netter, though now is in private hands. The steam herring drifter *Feasible* is sometimes around and a couple of Cornish luggers add to the eclectic collection, though it must be added that one of these was built purely as a pleasure boat on Cornish lugger lines. Though none of these vessels were built in or around Bristol, what they do have in common is the will to be based at or near the head of the Bristol Channel and as such they show that Bristol has the ability to become one of Britain's first nationally recognised historic harbours for such craft, under proposals being formulated by National Historic Ships. The priority is to establish three national centres to develop maritime skills and facilities under the titles of the Bristol Channel Network, the Medway Network and the Solent Network, with Bristol a focal point of the Bristol Channel Network which would also include a contribution from Gloucester, Sharpness and Cardiff.

Left: A bow view of *Pegasus* from the shed. She took about eighteen months to build.

Below: Launch day for *Pegasus* from the Redcliffe Boatyard in May 2008. As she is lifted over by crane she shows off her graceful lines. (Courtesy of Petros Kounouklas)

The fireboat *Pyronaut* showing off her hoses at the Bristol Harbour Festival in 2006. This weekend festival remains the largest free event in the West Country and attracts crowds from all over. Although the boats arrive from far afield and all sorts of stalls sell food, drink and other goods, sadly maritime heritage doesn't play a great part in the festivities.

Two vessels immediately associated with the port are Brunel's *Great Britain* and the replica of John Cabot's *Matthew*, built in Bristol and launched in 1996. But, more importantly, the vessels that identify with Bristol are the Bristol Channel pilot cutters, of which the *Peggy* is often moored along the quay, somewhere between the *Great Britain* and *Tangaroa*. Originally named *Wave*, she had been built by Edwin 'Cracker' Rowles, one of the two pilot cutter builders working at nearby Pill around 1900, the other being Cooper. Built for Richard Arthur Case, pilot number ten, he was unfortunately drowned a few years later while trying to board SS *Heartburn* off Nash Point. She was sold on, remaining a pilot boat until 1920, at which time she was renamed *Peggy* by Major C. Watson-Smyth, who also owned another cutter. In 1925 she was converted to a yacht by A.H. Moody & Son. Some twelve owners followed over the next four decades. In 1964 *Peggy* was bought by Alan Smith of Mylor; four years later she was bought by Alan Savage from Penarth, who replaced a few planks on a tired boat; then, in 1973, she was taken to Bristol and sold to local man Diccon Pridie who, with his wife Jan, sails her extensively each summer.

There are, of course, several other original pilot cutters still sailing, for similar craft were based in Newport, Cardiff and Barry Docks. Swansea, as we shall see in a subsequent

Bow of the new fishing boat *Girl Lauren* as she fast becomes a boat in the same shed that built *Mischief* and *Morwenna*.

chapter, developed a pilot cutter with a very different rig from the traditional gaff of the ones from up channel. Gloucester boatbuilder Tommi Nielsen has been responsible for restoring some whilst others are to be found in various corners. In actuality, there is no such thing as a Bristol Channel pilot cutter: it is a generic term. Even Peter Stuckey noted the difference when he titled his seminal book *The Sailing Pilots of the Bristol Channel*. Today there are seventeen 'original' pilot cutters that worked in the Bristol Channel at some time during their working life. Of these, five were built at Pill, just downstream from Bristol, four in South Wales (Newport and Cardiff), another four in Cornwall, two in Fleetwood and one each in Devon and Gloucester. No two vessels are the same, thus they are classified under their usage rather than similar hull shape as most craft are by today's academics. What they do have in common, other than usage, is their fine sailing abilities, deep hull and gaff rig. In fact, so popular are they as cruising and charter vessels that several 'new' pilot cutters have been built over the last few years, and Bristol has, quite rightly, been in the forefront of this revival of building these vessels in the traditional way.

The original 45ft pilot cutter *Mischief* was built by Thomas Baker of Cardiff in 1906 and in 1954 came into the hands of renowned explorer Bill Tilman who documented his adventures in his many books. Tilman sailed her over 100,000 miles to both the Arctic and Antarctic until she hit a rock and was subsequently crushed by ice off Jan Mayen

Sea trials in the harbour with the SS *Great Britain* towering behind.

The SS *Great Britain*, housed in the dry dock in which Brunel's boat was built, is today one of the top attractions in the whole country. Brought back from the Falkland Islands in 1970, she is in a permanent site and appears to be afloat although the public can go 'below the sea' to view the hull of the old iron boat.

Island in 1968. After that he sailed two other pilot cutters *Sea Breeze* (1968–1972) and *Baroque* (1973–1977), thus creating much of the lore about these craft. Tilman's exploits fascinated Bristol boatbuilder John Raymond-Barker of RB Boatbuilding, which resulted in him laying the keel of a replica of Tilman's *Mischief* at the Underfall Boatyard in Bristol. Initially using images of the original boat, and with the help of Ed Burnett and an excellent computer programme, the lines plan was developed from other Cardiff boats with similar lines, ratios and coefficients. The finished vessel was launched in November 2007 and has since been working as a charter vessel based in Western Scotland. Then, in April 2009, Raymond-Barker launched his second new pilot cutter *Morwenna* when she was officially named by Gloucestershire and England cricketer, and now famed artist, Jack Russell, amongst a fanfare of music and theatre with upwards of 200 onlookers. *Morwenna* was almost identical in hull shape, though with some subtle differences, to *Mischief*, though with a very different layout below the decks and now charters from her base in the Solent. His third vessel, a transom-sterned pilot cutter, is due for launching in 2011.

Another of the recently built pilot cutters running charters on the south coast is *Pegasus* which emerged from the Redcliffe Quay workshop of Bristol boatbuilder Mark Rolt in May 2008. Mark had been one of the principal boatbuilders working on the *Matthew* a decade or more before and had hankered after building a pilot cutter for several years.

'Isambard Kingdom Brunel' viewing the kippers in Kipperman's smokehouse in 2010. The *Great Britain*'s launch in 1843 coincided with the invention of the kipper in Seahouses, Northumberland. I bet he didn't know that!

When his chance came he chose a big version at 56ft in length, again a boat designed by Ed Burnett.

However, the first of the recent new breed of these pilot cutters was the *Polly Agatha*, built by Falmouth boatbuilders Cockwells Modern and Classic Boatbuilding and launched in 2007. The company is run by Dave Cockwell, who himself hails from Bristol and used to work out of the Underfall Yard. He once said that his early nurturing of a seed of boat construction came from father and son Denis and David Williams, and Bob James, all of Pill. *Polly Agatha* was modelled on *Peggy* after Dave took the lines off. His second pilot cutter, *Merlin*, was launched in the autumn of 2009 and is another set to work as a charter vessel.

The original pilot cutters were undoubtedly seaworthy vessels which developed through a suitability to the work they undertook. Pilots were needed wherever ships came into port, imparting their local knowledge of the local dangers to ensure the ships safely arrived and departed. To those using the port of Bristol, with its tidal approach, it was vital. The pilots had to cope with the unpredictable seas in which they often had to remain out for days searching for incoming ships. They normally waited around Lundy Isle until an approaching ship was hailed to gain its services and speed was often needed when in competition with another pilot cutter to reach a particular vessel. The cutters were crewed by a minimum crew of one man and a boy, the pilot himself not being part of the crew. Stories abound of the man acting as pilot so that the boy had to sail the boat home safely on his own. By the early 1900s the Bristol Channel pilot cutters had reached their perfection before steam and motorisation eventually made them obsolete in terms of work. That they were so seaworthy, even yacht-like in some ways, made them perfect for conversion into pleasure boats. Being roomy, they have subsequently become popular as charter vessels. Coupled with the recent trend to build using traditional wood materials and their associated skills, these, and other similar vessels such as the Scillonian pilot cutters, have once again come into their own.

The building of wooden fishing boats in Britain almost completely collapsed in the first years of the twenty-first century but, as always, there are exceptions. One of these is Bristol boatbuilder Tim Loftus, who in the summer of 2010 completed the build of a 24ft fishing boat for east coast of Scotland owners. The vessel, named *Girl Lauren*, was designed by the builder with input from the owner and the shape was influenced by similar boats the builder had seen on the west coast of Scotland.

6

THE STOP-NET FISHERS OF GATCOMBE

O f all the commercial fisheries in the Bristol Channel it is probably the salmon that first comes to most people's minds, which is a reflection of the fact that the river Severn was England's best-known salmon river. It is also probably the fish that has been the most widely written about, though of course it was not just confined to the Severn. Indeed, from the rivers Taw and Torridge of Devon and Somerset's Parrett (all of which I have already mentioned) to the many rivers of the Welsh valleys, salmon was an important means of a seasonal income for many fishermen. In the same way, various different forms of fishing were practised, some of which I have already glimpsed. The Severn itself runs for 220 miles from Plynlimon in Wales to approximately Severn Beach, after which it is deemed to become the Severn Estuary. After that a line from Lavernock Point, south of Cardiff, to Sand Point, near Weston-super-Mare, is generally regarded as being the boundary between the Estuary and the Bristol Channel. Furthermore it's tidal up to the weirs at Gloucester, though of course this was much further upstream before the weirs were built. Within this area of water are several methods of fishing for salmon which are mostly unique to the Severn and which have almost entirely ceased to operate today except in a minimal and non-profit-making way. Some, such as stop-netting, drift-netting and putt fishing have been consigned to the history books, whilst a few putcher ranks still survive, as do the Black Rock lave-net fishermen. The few folk still practising this ancient method wade into the river Severn on a falling tide with their handheld bag-net suspended on a Y-shaped wooden frame made from ash or willow. They then wait around, watching for a fish. When one is detected the fisherman attempts to intercept him by moving across the river and dipping his net in its path. Today there are only

Lave-net fisherman with his net on the Welsh side of the lower river Severn. (Courtesy of Black Rock Lave-Net Fishermen Association)

Another unknown lave-net fisherman at Minsterworth, on the upper Severn, with a good catch of salmon in the 1950s. The net was drawn in, otherwise the wily salmon could slip out of the fisherman's hands and make its escape.

A large rank of putchers on the east bank of the Severn in the 1930s. (Courtesy of Environment Agency)

seven members of the Black Rock Lave Net Fishermen's Association from around the Portskewett area where Black Rock is, and they fish at specific times in the season which are advertised on their website. They have a Net House in which there is an historical exhibition, part of their desire to promote and explain their ancient art. It is a place where they can repair their nets and await the tide.

Coracle fishing on the Severn has finished, though it does continue on several of the Welsh rivers such as the Towy and Teifi whilst a few drafts on the Severn are licensed for long nets to be used, the draft being the actual part of the river where this form of fishing can take place (as mentioned in Chapter 2) and which belongs to the owners of the riverbank.

From a personal experience point of view, the long-net is the only one of these methods of fishing I have taken part in although I have paddled my coracle whilst attempting to demonstrate coracle fishing. The latter involves two coracles with a net strung out between them as they drift downriver. It sounds simple but I assure you it's not, especially when attempting to demonstrate it on a lake!

As to long-netting, at one time these nets were used throughout the navigable part of the river above the point that the river narrows between Frampton and Awre right up to Welshpool. Today the three drafts that do still continue are situated between Bullo Pill and Gloucester. Prior to the 1860s the fishing was largely unregulated, though subsequent to a Special Commission for the Salmon Fisheries in 1866 increasing interference and control has reduced the time, method, place and extent of fishing to control stocks which were almost at a totally collapsed level twenty years ago. Today they are improved, though

A putt was a large so-called 'fixed engine' for fishing and consisted of three parts. It was also deadly, catching all fish down to shrimps. Wooden sticks were placed over the entrance to prevent salmon entering out of the salmon season. Compare the size of this one to the bull behind! (Courtesy of Environment Agency)

A combination rank of both putchers and putts in the river Severn. (Courtesy of Environment Agency)

Unknown couple with salmon in front of their putcher rank about 1920. They are possibly members of the Nash family and their rank was located around the area where the first Severn Crossing now stands. (Courtesy of Environment Agency)

A 1920s upriver-type punt at Minsterworth. Note how little sheer there is at the bow and stern. These were used mostly for eel fishing. The punts of the tidal part of the river were more shapely and designed to cope with the Severn bore.

Left: Ann Cooper aboard her long-net punt shooting the net in the recreation of Turner's painting of Worcester Cathedral. These punts were the main small working boats of the river and were used for fishing, ferrying and general transport. (Courtesy of Simon Cooper)

Below: Long-net fishing at Newnham. At least three of these coble-type boats were brought down from Berwick-upon-Tweed. They were designed and built specifically for the draft net and were found suitable to fish the river Severn.

angling supersedes any commercial fishing in terms of numbers of fish caught, although fishing can only take place between June and August, only during the week and daylight hours.

A long net is a net around 90 yards long and 4 yards in depth, although longer nets up to 200 yards are used where the river is wider. According to one regulation – and there are plenty covering all forms of fishing in the river, such as designating times of fishing, size of the net, and so on – the net should only reach out over three quarters of the width of the river. It is fished like a seine net in that one end is fed out into the river by boat whilst the other end is held ashore. This job on the river bank is that of the person

Hauling in the net after a shot at Bollo Pill, near Minsterworth, in 2003. Simon Cooper is on the right. Bollo Pill has not been fished since 2007. (Courtesy of Simon Cooper)

known as the debut-man, who holds one line – the debut-line – which is attached to the head and footropes of the net. The headrope is buoyed with floats whilst the footrope is weighted with lead sinkers. Once the sturdy flat-bottomed boat – traditionally named a long-net punt – is rowed out into the river and downstream with the net being paid out in a semi-circular fashion, the debut-man walks along the river bank in the same direction. Once the net is almost all out the punt is rowed back to the shore but at some distance downstream and the fourth member of the team jumps ashore with the another line – the muntle – which is itself attached to that end of the net. This fellow then is the muntle-man. Thus once both lines are ashore these are pulled in, bringing in the net, and eventually the debut-man reaches the muntle-man to close the net before the other two in the punt jump ashore and they all haul the ends of the two lines to a windlass on the bank which is then used to draw in the whole net. The whole operation takes about an hour and fishing starts about two hours after high water, enabling the fishermen to fish four drafts before low water four hours later. These days only the occasional salmon is caught this way whereas a century ago this was a deadly fishing method. Traditionally any fish caught other than salmon can be claimed by the debut-man. We only caught one salmon the day I took part!

But it is the fishers of Gatcombe that interest us most here. Not that there are many of them: just a handful. Gatcombe itself, hidden from the outside world, almost sits astride the river, on its northern side, a bit north-east of Lydney and upstream of Sharpness

A group of Severn fishermen and other river folk outside former riverside inn the Sloop at Bollo Pool. In addition to the fishing crews of the Severn, trows would stop at the sloop as they worked with the tide to move upriver. (Courtesy of Jim Gleed)

The Sloop Inn, Gatcombe, out of the salmon season. The tide is very high and had flooded the grass in front of the pub and the stop-net boats have been pulled right up away from the water. (Mike Smylie Collection)

on the opposite bank. Here the river has opened up after its various bends down from Gloucester and long-nets are no longer able to be used because of the exposure to the weather rolling in directly from the south-west. From this point, and downstream, the fishers use the stop-nets.

The stop-net has more romance attached to it than the long-net and other ways of fishing, even if it is a more dangerous occupation. Why there is this romantic notion attached to the fishery is unclear, but suggestions as to how this came about include the fishermen's shrewdness in outwitting the fish in his elements, the fact that they fish alone, in silence, for several hours at a time or because the net itself looks almost antiquated and thus there is a sentimentality attached to it. I guess it wasn't the fishermen who dreamt up these fanciful ideas, because it was simple plain hard work out there and presumably it was onlookers who visualised the fishermen alone in their boats fighting nature, both in terms of the weather and the fish.

Both methods – long-net and stop-net – were equally skilful in their successful prosecution, though in reality the lave-net was probably the most skilful of all the various methods of pitting one's wits against the salmon and the elements. To operate a stop-net one must first have a stop-net boat, a sturdy vessel, heavily built and sometimes called a stopping boat. Each fisherman had his own boat which he sculled out to the fishing ground. Between 1866 and 1870 there were something like twenty-four stop-nets authorised on the river Severn with more than that number registered on the river Wye. Nowhere else is this method practised, though something similar developed in west Wales, as we will discover in Chapter 8.

The stop-net itself was a bag net suspended on two 24ft-long pieces of stout Norwegian spruce called 'rames'. These are held in a 'V' by a spreader whilst weights at the apex of

A river Wye stop-net boat having just landed a salmon. Note the heavy fibre net and mooring pole to which the boat is attached at the bow.

Three stop-net boats fishing in Wellhouse Bay all on the same mooring wire. Two have their nets down whilst the nearest has his raised. (Courtesy of Environment Agency)

the frames complete the frame. Once the stop-net boat was moored fore and aft to its 'chain', one of the many wire warps lying perpendicular to the stream attached to a stake ashore and anchored in deep water, broadside on to the river, the frame was lowered into the tide so that the bag opened up below the boat. Hence the shallow draft of the vessel and lack of much of a skeg which would both entangle the net and create more drag as the boat sits across the current. Five feeling strings were attached to different parts of the net and to a 'tuning fork' – a wooden stick – which was held by the fisherman. A wooden prop supported the weighted apex. Once a fish was detected through vibrations in one of the feeling wires which resonated into the stick, the fisherman kicked the prop out – called 'knocking out' – and helped by his weight the net came up out of the water with, hopefully, the fish still in. If so, this was extracted through the 'cunning hole' which, when untied, was a concealed entrance to the cod end where the fish ended up. A quick thump with the 'knobbling pin' consigned the fish to the thereafter and the net was again tied up and dropped back into the water, propped up to await another unfortunate fish. When the fishing was good several salmon could be landed during the three hours of fishing, though when the tide was strong or the water calm they might get nothing.

They have been stop-netting from Gatcombe for generations. Although now a sleepy hamlet of a few houses, this was once a busy port. Today the only access to the river is below one of the archways of the embankment carrying the Gloucester and South Wales railway line but before that was built in 1854 trade was thriving. Two pubs once served the local community: the Sloop and Ship Inns. The former is now Drake's House, because Francis Drake is reputed to have stayed there when sourcing timber for shipbuilding from the Forest of Dean. Walter Raleigh is said to have visited for the same reason and the Spanish, so the story goes, hatched a plan to burn the entire forest to thwart Britain's shipbuilding plans but they failed miserably. The Ship Inn was home to the Morse family after it was purchased by Charles Morse in 1878, though it had already ceased to be an inn and had had its name changed to Court House, as that was where the rents were paid on properties owned by the Duchy of Etloe.

Before the Morses purchased the house, it had been home to William and Sarah Shaw and William's brother Thomas, and the two brothers were the operators of the stop-net

A close-up of the working space of a stop-net boat. The net is drying. Note the weights on the frames to counterbalance the weight of the net in the water. The canvas sheet is to protect the fisherman from the worst of the wind. (Courtesy of Environment Agency)

One of the three last stop-net boats to have fished through the later part of the twentieth century, moored by the railway wall in the 1980s. (Courtesy of Environment Agency)

Above: A fully restored example of a Wye type of stopping boat. Wye stopping boats were shorter and of less beam than the boats located at Gatcombe. However boats from the Wye fisheries fished in a number of locations on the Severn. This boat would have once had a sail to propel to out to the fishing ground. (Courtesy of Simon Cooper)

Left: A fisherman from Littleton on the east bank of the Severn clearing the weed from his net in the 1920s. Sometimes it was only seaweed and other debris that these nets caught. Note the waders he is wearing, because if someone falls over the side in those, it's straight to the bottom without much chance of survival.

The same fisherman at Littleton. Note the ropes and pulley to lift the net out of the water, unlike the Gatcombe boats which used counterweights.

Four Gatcombe fishermen with the day's catch.

fishery. Tragically William was drowned in 1878 when the stopping boat he was in with his brother and local fisherman Thomas Margate hit the nearly completed Severn railway bridge which was under construction between Sharpness and Purton. The boat sank though the other two survived and the lease of the fishery passed to Thomas. William's body, incidentally, was taken to the Sloop Inn when it was recovered from the river after it was found upon a sandbank on the Sharpness side, which suggests the inn, at least, was still operating as a drinking house.

Stop-netting is said to predate the Civil War in the seventeenth century and is thought to have evolved from the lave-net. Documented evidence informs us that in the 1640s Royalist Sir John Wintour of Lydney was ferried across the river Wye in a stop-net boat whilst being pursued by Parliamentary forces. Subsequent to that information is sparse until the 1866 Special Commission when evidence was taken to establish fishing rights in law. At that time Thomas Shaw, William and Thomas' father, had been the tenant of the fishery for forty years after he had bought it from George Shaw. The elder Thomas was also a shipwright who built several local barges, known as trows, as well as probably the stop-net boats used there.

The 'chains' were situated both off Gatcombe and in nearby Wellhouse Bay, the former belonging to the Crown at the Highgrove Estate whilst Lord Bledisloe of Lydney owned the latter. Gatcombe was considered the most dangerous and when a fisherman named Fenner drowned there in 1937 fishing ceased. Prior to that there were ten stop-net boats at Gatcombe in total though after 1937 it was restricted to the seven chains in Wellhouse Bay named thus: Haywards Rock, two at Long Ledge, Round Rock, Fish House, Old Dunns and The Flood. Six boats were able to tie up to one chain and the wind and tide dictated which of these were the best for any one tide.

There were more stop-net fisheries along the river at Lydney, Berkeley, Hill Pill and Croome Hill, the latter three being on the southern side of the river. In total there were twenty-four licences whilst on the river Wye there were a further thirteen licences to fish

The season ended with the fishermen hauling the boats out at Gatcombe. They were firstly manhandled from the river... (Courtesy of Ann Bayliss)

some forty locations up as far as Monmouth, another twenty-three below Chepstow and fourteen in Beachley Bay just upstream on the river Severn. Stop-netting was a popular and effective way of catching the salmon.

1986, though, was the final year, when the last of the stop-netters went out to fish. By that time it was Charles Morse's great-great-granddaughter Ann who leased the rights and she was married to the last fisher Raymond Bayliss. When I met Ann and Raymond in the late 1990s they were anxious to pass on their story of the fishing and they showed me the records of the fishing stretching back two generations, all in leather-bound volumes whose pages illustrate the pride and thoroughness with which the fishing was run. In an exquisite, almost copperplate, style every aspect of the business is captured in these pages. Sadly both have now passed on, though I still remember vividly the images of that day, etched as they are onto the notebook in my head.

The 'salmon accounts' detailed each fish caught, its weight and selling price, whilst the 'wages book' stated the earnings of each stop-net fisherman they employed. One volume named each of the lave-net fishermen they employed as there was also a lave-net fishery here, as well as giving the number of salmon so caught. Another small book listed his annual expenditure and each was a time capsule into that era that even today leaves us with a glimpse of how the fishery was operated and how much an average fisherman earned.

In 1913, for example, the average wage was 8s per 10lb of salmon caught with each fish weighing within the range 10–20lb. The record for a salmon caught in a stop-net was, I discovered, 62lb, though this was caught a few years later than 1913. In February 1913 an average fish fetched 2s 3d, reducing to 1s 6d in March and 1s 2d in July. The fishermen received about half of this and the Morses the other half, out of which they paid all the rents, licences, boat and net costs and transportation. In total 1,179 salmon were caught

...before they were dragged to their winter home and chocked up. Then it was back to Court House for cold salt beef, beetroot and mashed potato, apple pie and oodles of cider. (Courtesy of Ann Bayliss)

during that season that commenced on 2 February and continued right through until its closure on 15 August. It was a much longer season in those times. Total sales for that year were just over £1,070 with the expenses at about £646, giving a total profit of almost £424. A licence in 1893 cost £3 which had risen to £12 by 1961. In 1932, as another example, the telephone bill was nearly £16, repairs to the boats £40, three stop-nets £6, insurance about £16, rent to Highgrove £15 and to Lord Bledisloe £30. Sales that year had increased to £1,411 and expenditure £1,147 with a reduced profit of £254. Some years produced losses which were often counteracted by bumper years. In some respects things never change.

At that visit Ann Bayliss showed us around her outside workshop. Here, as a child, she explained how she helped her father set up the nets, for, like Brendan Sellick in Stolford and most other inshore fishermen, he made up his own nets. These were made from hemp before 1965 with the raw material coming from Bridport in panels 76ft long by 30ft deep. The top 3ft of the finished net had a 7in mesh, decreasing every 2ft to 6, 5 and 4½in, to finally 4in for the last 18ft of net. Together they would knit the various meshes into one net. The mesh pins, wooden needles and the wooden winder were still there amongst the boatbuilding tools, almost like the exhibits in a museum, though this was no museum. On the lid of a chest were two lists still hanging, dated 1899 and 1923, containing the names of the fishermen of those years, the particular stopping boat they used and the size of net they required. It was as if nothing had been touched in a century and a half expected her father to walk in at any moment to begin work on a net.

Once the net had been completed it was carried outside and tarred in the copper boiler that was still sitting there outside the blacksmith's shop. Tarring, or barking as it was called, ensured the nets didn't rot in the salty water. Immersed nets would stay in the mixture of tar and tar oil for several days before they were hauled out on the pulley that was suspended above and left to drip. Then they were hung up to dry thoroughly. Nets seldom lasted more than a season so they were only barked at the beginning.

The stopping boats they used were built specifically for stop-netting and were 26ft long and 7ft in beam. They had the minimum of keel as already mentioned to reduce the sideways drag when moored to the chain and to prevent the net being obstructed underneath. They were heavily constructed with oak frames and larch and elm planking. Gunwales were ash to cope with the stresses of the frame of the net. Other than a grey strip above the rubbing strake, they were pitched inside and out.

I remember Ann describing how her father and fisherman Joe Wathen had built the last boat in 1922. This was the *Margaret*, No.30, and at that time this was one of the three boats lying rotting away on the grassy slope close to the railway arch through which the boats were launched. They were still there even three years ago, though I haven't checked since. Sadly, though, they were just shells the last time I looked, covered in brambles and nettles and I wouldn't be surprised if they had disappeared the next time I look, cleared away by some unsuspecting person who has no idea as to their vintage. The timber, Ann had said, came from the sawmills at the edge of the Forest of Dean, chosen by Charles Morse (her grandfather) himself. It had taken about three months to build this boat, which was named after her father's youngest sister.

Repairs were likewise undertaken outside the workshop after the season's close. This was the time of bringing the boats in. On an August high tide, just after the full moon, all ten boats were dragged up under the railway line, one by one, with the help of horses and all the fishermen and their families. This day became a celebration of the salmon fishing, a form of thanksgiving after a successful annual harvest from the river. Once each boat had been blocked up to dry out, everyone went up to Court House for a meal of cold salt beef, beetroot and mashed potato, followed by homemade apple pie, all accompanied by ample supplies of cider and fishermen's stories that rolled on and on…

Winter was also the time to earn a living outside of the fishing. The Morse family undertook general carpentry repairs and made ladders to sell. Then there was plum-picking and cider-making. They had cows that needed milking and calves that had to be tended. Ann remembered milking the fourteen cows and taking the churns to the top of the lane to await collection by Cadbury's. Her grandfather on her mother's side looked after the lights on the Severn Railway bridge whilst her father also ran the local Blakeney Gas, Light & Coke Company. Also in winter the galvanised cables in the river needed relaying and, at that visit, I read a note in the carpenter's shed dated 1915 that noted their lengths: 'Length of slack wire: 40 fathom, Gatcombe: 83 [fathom], Fish House Head: 73, Low Water Wire: 45, Middle: 83, Dunns: 65.' The Fish House referred to was situated at Wellhouse Bay and had been a small stone building with two rooms, one with bunks, cupboards and a fireplace and the other a storeroom for fishing gear. Here the fishermen would sit around the open fire or sleep, waiting for the right state of tide to begin fishing. When the house was destroyed in a very high tide in 1950, Charles Morse built a wooden shed higher up the railway embankment. Sadly, like the fishery, this too has disappeared.

The lasting memory I have of Raymond was of slicing up his home-cured bacon which he gave to me. That was just another of his subsistence occupations; meat that he sold. His and Ann's life together was one of combining river work with that of the land, like many other fishers today. In the same way that Adrian Sellick in Stolford works at night in the yogurt factory or Tom Smith in Sunderland Point (see my last book *Fishing Around Morecambe Bay*) works long hours in his vegetable garden, longshore fishing has for many been this mixture for many generations. With Ann and Raymond's passing on, yet another tradition has disappeared and before long they will all have gone. Gone everywhere throughout these islands.

7

COCKLES AND OYSTERS –
THE FISHERIES OF SWANSEA
AND CARMARTHEN BAY

Geographically speaking, Carmarthen Bay can be said to stretch from Caldey Island in the west to Worm's Head, the western tip of the Gower Peninsula, in the east, and is much larger than Swansea Bay. It also includes the expanse of the Burry Inlet. Swansea Bay, the water between Mumbles Head at its western periphery to some indeterminate spot east of what is now the city of Swansea, though much the smaller of the two bays, was nevertheless edged by a thriving maritime fringe even before the copper smelters and coal exports developed Swansea into one of the most important British ports.

Fishing is indeed an age old profession there and in the late eighteenth century a fish market was popular with local bounties paid by 'common attorneys' to invigorate the business. Thus 4s a hundredweight was paid on the landing of most fishes including turbot, John Dory and soles whilst lesser fishes got 1s. A mease of herring or 500 mackerel attracted a 1s bounty too. However these levels of bounties didn't last long and were halved the following year in 1793 and soon abolished. By 1808 the trade in fish was described as having 'increased'. A century later Swansea was a steam trawler port and in 1904 the Castle fleet of trawlers moved from Milford. The fishing grounds were out to the west though some vessels fished as far away as Ilha Berlenga, abreast of Portugal.

Much of Swansea's growth prior to the first mutterings of the harbour development was due to a healthy abundance of oysters in the deeper waters of the bay and off Mumbles Head. Oysters had for centuries been a vital export for South Wales and it is believed the

'Fishing the Weir, Swansea' by Edward Duncan, 1847. Swansea Bay was the centre of various fisheries such as oysters at the Mumbles, otherwise known as Oystermouth. (Mike Smylie Collection)

Romans were fond of these molluscs. In the late sixteenth century, according to the *Welsh Port Books*, a consignment of 20,000 oysters was exported from Tenby. Milford Haven, as we shall see in the next chapter, was plentiful in oysters of a fine flavour at this time. By the seventeenth century the Swansea Bay oyster fishery was centred upon the small village of Oystermouth, tucked under Mumbles Head and the oyster landed there was said to be the best in Britain. Whether this was a biased opinion remains to be seen though it has to be said there is seldom a fishery in the country that someone hasn't declared as being the best in Britain!

Harvesting was by dredging using a small open boat, crewed by three men, stoutly built and usually rowed – a small skiff indeed, about 25ft in length and built locally. This vessel would tow a dredge that scraped along the bottom of the seabed with the oysters being caught in a net trailing behind the iron framework. As the boats the fishermen were able to purchase grew in size, more than one dredge could be towed and four crew became the norm. Eventually, by the middle of the nineteenth century, the oyster skiff developed into a sailing vessel of about 35ft, at first still undecked though some began to appear as half-decked craft. These vessels rigged two shallop sails – lug sails rigged on steeply raking masts similar to the schooner rig, a rig uncommon around the British Isles, though thought to have come from the wherry rig further to the north – and sometimes a headsail. As the town and port of Swansea developed, when pilot boats were needed

Left: Fish weirs also were in use in Carmarthen Bay, this one lying on the east side of the bay and still being visible today.

Below: Oyster skiffs lying at anchor off Oystermouth, probably in the 1880s. Some of the smaller boats were also used for dredging under sail or oar. (Mike Smylie Collection)

to bring shipping into the river avoiding the offshore shoals, it was this rig that was ultimately favoured.

The size of the oyster trade can be illustrated by the size of the catch. Just over nine million oysters were taken in 1873 though the trade was said to be in decline. Indeed, in terms of the number of vessels, the trade is said to have peaked in 1871 when 188 boats were engaged in the fishery. By 1875 the amount of oysters taken had shrunk to a third of that of four years earlier. By 1894 a meagre 600,000 were taken. In an industry that employed over 140 skiffs in the middle of the nineteenth century there was a sharp downfall from that time onwards. This was said to be because of overfishing, primarily because of the influx of boats from the east coast of England – chiefly from Colchester and Whitstable, though some also came from Jersey – who were renowned for their sailing long distances for oysters to seed their overfished beds. Much of what they fished was spat for their reseeding, though they also dredged mature oysters. The locals were

Although many of the larger smacks working the oyster beds came from the east coast of England, some such as these two – *Snake* and *Hawk* – were built in Appledore. (Mike Smylie Collection)

A typical Tenby lugger, M172, under full sail off Tenby. (Courtesy of Tenby Museum)

Tenby Harbour in the 1890s. The local luggers are moored in front whilst almost all the smacks behind are registered in either Dartmouth (DH) or Brixham (BM). (Mike Smylie Collection)

Horse and carts making their way down onto Burry sands, bringing with them the cockle pickers. (Mike Smylie Collection)

Travelling out onto the sands, the pickers, mostly women, start work as soon as the tide allows access to the cockle sands. (Mike Smylie Collection)

unable to compete with their smaller boats so they began to purchase larger smacks on the same lines as the east coast smacks. Thus the older skiffs were phased out and the newer type of gaff-rigged Mumbles oyster skiffs appeared, complete with topsails and foresails. Some were brought in from the east coast whilst others were ordered from boatbuilders across in Appledore, North Devon, for about £300. Some even came in from Cornish boatbuilders though, seemingly, none were built locally whereas many were fitted out, repaired and annually overhauled at the Mundick yard that existed on Oystermouth's beach between 1860 and 1892.

As the boats became bigger they were able to sail further afield so that, instead of merely dredging in the grounds in the bay and those known as the 'Roads Haul' and 'White Oyster Ledge', both off Mumbles Head, they were working the beds off the Helwick shoals and 'Metz Haul' off Porthcawl. Oysters were then brought ashore and kept fresh in 'perches' – areas marked out for individual fishermen – within Swansea Bay until taken to market.

By 1914 there were only fourteen skiffs still engaged in oysters and one commentator observed that the 'fisher folk there devote themselves almost exclusively to that business'. By then the foreign boats had departed and the locals were left to fish what remained. By that time it was, ironically, the Mumbles fishermen who were sailing north up to the Solway Firth in search of the shellfish. They had already fished off Tenby, as we shall soon see. Industrial and sewage pollution from an expanding Swansea brought disease after

Above: Cockle-picking is lonely and back-breaking labour. (Mike Smylie Collection)

Left: Once collected, the cockles have to be riddled to get rid of the sand and to make sure no undersize cockles are taken. (Mike Smylie Collection)

the end of the First World War and by 1925 all activity had stopped. Only three of the Mumbles fleet survived – the sailing skiff *Emmeline*, 14SA, built by William Paynter of St Ives in 1865 and the two motorised skiffs *Secret* and *Rising Sun*. Within several years they'd gone too.

A small fleet of similar boats were based in the tiny haven of Port Eynon on the Gower Peninsula where there were said to be forty small skiffs working in the 1840s and twenty-two larger vessels in 1864. By 1879 the industry had closed though it is probable

The women then return from their work and the cockles are taken away. Here some of them carry their riddles on their heads. (Mike Smylie Collection)

Today's cocklers use very different machinery to carry the cockles. Here the view over the river Towy estuary captured the 4x4 vehicles they use nowadays.

that, because of the lack of decent shelter at Port Eynon, any local boats would base themselves around at Oystermouth.

It is strange how the type of fishing boat used in two areas not more than twenty miles apart developed completely separately into two very distinctively different craft. The Oystermouth men had their skiffs modelled on east coast boats after abandoning their earlier transom-sterned open boats whilst at Tenby, the centre of the Carmarthen Bay oyster fishery, they retained their transom sterns and developed their own lugger. Thus what is known now as the 'Tenby lugger' became the all-purpose fishing boat for oyster dredging, herring drifting, long-lining, potting for lobsters and crabs and, in the summer season, for taking trippers out around the bay or to Caldey Island once visitors started coming to Tenby in the very late eighteenth century.

Tenby was once the most important fishing station in Wales where huge amounts of herring were landed. Indeed its name in Welsh, *Dinbych-y-pysgod*, literally means 'little fort of the fishes' and it was one of the first places in the Principality to have a quay built

The method of picking hasn't changed very much over the years. The cockles are still collected by hand, here at Ferryside with Llansteffan Castle on the opposite bank.

when Edward III funded one in 1328 for the 'good men of Teneby'. Tithes of herrings and oysters were paid for mass to be said on their behalf at the small St Julian's Chapel which still sits on the harbour. Oysters were obviously as prolific as the herring and, as seen above, Tenby was exporting oysters in the sixteenth century. As in Swansea it was a fishery that was to continue until the nineteenth-century fishers began over-exploiting it.

The oysters here were generally on two grounds. One lay between Tenby and Caldey whilst the Stackpole beds were several miles further west off Stackpole Head, in deeper exposed water. Both these grounds produced a large variety of oyster which gave them a very strong taste and they were said to be mostly used in cooking as against eaten raw. Some were pickled locally and sent to the London market, whilst much of the fresh catch was exported to Bristol and Liverpool. Cooking oysters was much more common

Although hand raking is still preferred, some still use jumbos to tamp the sand to suck the cockles to the surface. However many people believe this tamping process destroys the cockles' natural habitat.

Raking with a 'cramm' was the normal implement, though this fellow seems to be using a cut-off garden rake.

The cockles are then bagged in 50kg sacks before being taken away for processing.

before the second half of the twentieth century when oysters became the darling of gastronomy and, accordingly, fetched much higher prices. This was partly due to the limited amount available because of overfishing but was, at the same time, a fashion in upmarket restaurants possibly encouraged by the aphrodisiac properties oysters are supposed to possess!

The Tenby luggers were half-decked luggers, clinker-built at first until carvel construction encouraged larger, heavily built boats. Most were around 25ft in length and they had upright stems, long keels and raking transom sterns. The rig consisted of a dipping lug mainsail, a much smaller mizzen spritsail, sheeted to an outrigger and a foresail set on a bowsprit. In 1864 up to thirty luggers were working and numbers seemed never to exceed fifty at any time at all. Brixham trawlers fished locally, as did the Swansea oyster skiffs and, possibly, east coast smacks, so that the oyster beds were soon overfished. A few Tenby fishermen brought in larger craft from Brixham and nearby Mumbles – becoming known as Tenby cutters – though these were short-lived. By the late 1800s the majority of the beds were almost empty and only a few of the local luggers continued fishing. Instead of dredging up 3,000 oysters they only brought home a few hundred. These boats persevered up to the 1940s though after the war the last of the old luggers seemed to have disappeared from the harbour though one, the *Seahorse*, survived in museum hands and awaits restoration. This vessel was built by James Newt about 1886 as the *Three Sisters* and, after her lines were take off in the 1930s and survived, it was decided the time was ripe to build a replica vessel in Milford Haven (see Chapter 9). Visitors still flock to Tenby and the local fishermen are busy ferrying them over to Caldey in the summer to visit the monks. But the days of the winter oyster fishery seem long gone.

Cockle fishing, on the other hand, still thrives, though diarrhetic shellfish poisoning and other natural occurrences affect the prevalence of the shellfish and the fishery remains closed for much of the time, only opening when it is deemed sensible. Like the oyster, though, it is a fishery that goes back a long time.

George Owen mentions cockles, amongst other shellfish, as being collected in Pembrokeshire in the late sixteenth century. When they were first harvested in the Burry Inlet will probably never be known for it must have been centuries ago. The first documented evidence seems to come from D.C. Davies who gave a paper to the

Cockles are small bivalves and it takes a fair amount of picking to fill one sack. Nevertheless there always seem plenty of people keen to get out and pick. Nowadays it has become a more regulated industry than it used to be.

Liverpool National Eisteddfod in 1884 and who noted that 'some five hundred families find employment; and the cockles and mussels taken are valued at over £15,000 a year. One little village, it is said, passes £2,000 a year through the Post Office'. Much of the catch was taken to the market at Swansea where the cockle sellers, women in flowing Welsh costume, were well known. Others went selling house-to-house, carrying baskets on their heads. Local lore has it that they walked in bare feet until reaching a particular bridge on the outskirts of Swansea, at which point they put on their best, and only, pair of boots.

In 1910 there were 250 pickers and these were almost exclusively women from the surrounding villages of Penclawdd, Crofty, Llanmorlais, Gowerton and Loughor – probably even the same women who sold the catch. They used a small rake or *cramm* which had seven prongs, a small knife and a sieve. Net-bags were used at one time but banned in 1996 in favour of rigid sieves. Today little has changed and only hand raking is allowed.

There are in fact two cockle fisheries under the jurisdiction of the South Wales Sea Fisheries Committee (SWSFC) after it was given the powers in 1965. The first, the Burry Inlet fishery, is carefully regulated with fifty-two licences being sold each year to, firstly, those fishing the previous year, and then any remaining to those on a waiting list that, a few years ago, had 180 people on it, proving the popularity of the fishery even if a licence cost £684 about five years ago. The fishery, which covers the area of the inlet between

Pamela Preston has been running her stall on the Carmarthen market for a number of years. Cockles and laverbread still remain popular foods in South Wales.

Swansea's fishing vessels are today squeezed into a small quay in the river Tawe, close to the sea lock, whereas once they commanded a decent home in the basin before the South Dock where there was a large fish market. Before that fishing craft were based in what was described as 'a little corner' of the larger Prince of Wales Dock.

Loughor Bridge and Pembrey Harbour, is open all year round, except for Sundays and at night. Each person has a daily quota of between 250–350kg, depending on the level of stocks and other factors determined by the authority.

The other area is called the 'Three Rivers', these rivers being the Towy, Taf and Gwendraeth, and is the area north of line between Tywyn Point in the east and Ginst Point. Again there is a history of fishing in this area with, in 1910, 150 people active at Ferryside, fifty at Laugharne, fifty at St Ishmaels and twelve at Llansteffan. Matheson gives a landing figure of 9,949cwt at Laugharne, worth £1,741 in 1925 and 25,905cwt at Ferryside worth £4,532.

Today, however, unlike the Burry Inlet fishery, this is a public fishery so all that is needed is a no-cost permit from the SWSFC on demand and they have no powers to charge even an administration fee for these permits. Up to 1998, the Three Rivers cockle fishery was extremely important in terms of the amount of molluscs fished. The minimum size for both these fisheries is that cockles must be unable to pass through a sieve of 19mm by 19mm mesh. Jumbos – wooden platforms attached to handles that were rocked on the sand to create suction and thus bring the cockle to the surface – were at one time used at Ferryside, although the Committee prefer to see hand raking as the only means of gathering the fish. The practice didn't seem to last that long although, technically, their use is not illegal. Because of the different nature of the sand, and the fact that the tidal range is lower, the only assumption is that they are not as effective here as they are in other parts of Britain. J. Geraint Jenkins shows a hand-pulled cockle dredge in use at the west side of Carmarthen Bay in the 1950s with some success, and another unsuccessful attempt was made to reintroduce this form of dredging into the Llanelli beds in the mid-1960s.

Cockles are processed locally and Selwyn's Penclawdd Seafoods, in their new factory right upon the shore that was opened by Her Majesty the Queen and the Duke of Edinburgh in May 1999, are one of the main processors. The business stems from the present owner's grandmother, Sarah Jones, who collected cockles in the nineteenth century and whose husband died of the dust from the coalmines. Her son Selwyn, seven years old, helped her at the time. As he grew up, Selwyn saw the potential of selling cockles further afield than the Swansea market and in time made a reputation for himself in selling good-quality cockles. Today his son Brian and daughter-in-law Alyson run the business that is now named after Selwyn. Once delivered, the cockles are washed, boiled and shelled before being taken to retail outlets and wholesale merchants throughout Britain, with a large amount being exported to the continent. And, at the end of this journey, the proof was in the pudding for Alyson produced some of the sweetest and tastiest cockles I'd ever tasted. Not for no reason do they insist that the Burry Inlet cockles are the best! And, incidentally, they go hand in hand with another delicacy from these parts: that of laver bread, locally picked seaweed which is cooked until soft and said to resemble a jelly. It's full of protein, iodine and vitamins and fried with cockles in bacon fat is a traditional Welsh meal. Superb!

8

THE LEGENDS OF LLANGWM

There was a time when unwary strangers visiting the small village of Llangwm (pronounced locally as Langum) on the west side of the Cleddau River would be met by a volley of carefully aimed stones to prevent their entry. Although this tradition probably stemmed from a cholera outbreak in the middle of the nineteenth century and was their way of keeping what was believed to be carriers of the disease at bay, the legend of stoning persisted into the twentieth century. Today's visitors are generally accepted with open arms, though there is still a degree of insularism said to originate from their Flemish and Norse ancestry.

They were certainly a very different community of people than would have been found in the vicinity, especially around the waterway where communities on the whole mingled and traded. The people of Llangwm were fishers and whilst the men collected the fruits of the sea and tended their boats and nets, it was left to the women to travel around the surrounding countryside to sell the products. These were enterprising and hard-working women who would walk many miles each day hawking their selection of fish: salmon, sewin (sea trout), herring, oysters, shrimps, cockles and other fish, depending on the fishing season. They would leave early in the morning and would travel as far as Carmarthen which meant a row across the river to Landshipping Quay. For the journey to Pembroke and Tenby, they would catch the Burton Ferry on Tuesdays and Fridays. They were easily identifiable by their unusual dress of flowing aprons, short red petticoats, heavy skirt, waist-length man's jacket and colourful shawl, with stout footwear on their feet. The fish was carried in a pannier on their back weighing a hundredweight or so when full and a small basket would be carried with samples of the fish available. Few had donkeys to help with the load. In more recent times they also sold their homemade butter

The quiet village of Llangwm in the 1930s with two small boats drawn up. It appeared a tranquil place. (Mike Smylie Collection)

whilst they supplied the Bristol market with pickled mussels and cockles. Nineteenth-century writers were indeed impressed with these unique women and thus they are well documented. One particular woman, Mary Palmer, was even featured in the *Daily Mail*. By the middle of the twentieth century, though they continued selling their wares, most adapted 'normal' dress and with increased choice for transportation, none had to walk the same long distances.

The men were equally hard working. Fishing occupied much of their life and shellfish had to be collected. The Milford Haven oysters were 'most delicate', according to George Owen when writing in 1603, and he also added that the chief places of their taking was at Lawrenny, Llangwm, the Pill and the Crow. Furthermore he tells us that they were dredged:

with a kind of iron made with bars, having a piece of horse or bullock skin sewn to it like a bag, in such sort as that it being fastened to a rope's end, is cast into the bottom of Milford at eight or ten fathoms, and is dragged at a boat's end by two rowers which row up and down the channel. And so the bag of leather, being made apt to scrape up all manner of things lying in the bottom, gathers up the oysters that breed there over certain known beds, which bag being filled they draw up and empty their oysters into their boat, applying their labour so all day, and when they have done they row to some appointed place near the shore at full sea and there cast out the oysters in a great heap, which they call beds, where every tide overflows them, and so are kept for lading boats to Bristol and other places.

At one time the Llangwm men fished at the Crow, otherwise known as Pennar Mouth, the earliest-known major source of oyster, where they carried them back to their maturing beds off Black Tar Point before being picked and sent off to market, either hawked locally or by smack to the English ports. One eyewitness report tells of 'as many as fifty coastal vessels beached at Guildford (Llangwm) to collect barrels of oysters which were shipped to Holland and other parts of the world'.

In the early nineteenth century a new way of fishing for salmon was introduced into Llangwm and nearby Hook whereas previously the fishermen had set seine-nets out from the shore. Two men from the Forest of Dean, Ormond (some call him Osmond) and Edwards, had come to work at the Landshipping coal mine and brought with them the stop-net technique from the rivers Severn and Wye. Adapting the method slightly to

Nevertheless fishing had played an important role in the development of the place, though I'm not sure I'd want to meet this family in the dead of the night. (Mike Smylie Collection)

Cockle women walked many miles selling the day's catch. (Mike Smylie Collection)

Their clothing was particularly noticeable with their tall black bonnets, aprons and flowing dresses and coats. (Mike Smylie Collection)

suit the river conditions, the method became known as the compass-net, though why is still unclear. Most seem to think it is so called because it resembles a huge draughtsman's compass with a net in the middle, though others disagree. The conditions on these three rivers were similar in that they were fast-flowing and tidal, yet the Cleddau was shallower which necessitated a smaller net working out of a smaller boat. Thus the compass-net boat was born.

Some of the Llangwm men, when not out fishing, worked in the naval dockyard at Pembroke Dock and it is said they carried the timber back with which they built their stout oak boats necessary for their fishing. Some were even built at the dockyard when work was slack. With reports stating that 100 boats were at times seen on the river, not surprisingly others were built by two boatbuilders based at Coheston. The boats were

Above: The boat on the left appears to be about to depart to the fishing, probably to drift-net judging by the net he has in the boat. (Simon Cooper Collection)

Left: Two compass-net boats at work on the upper reaches of the West Cleddau. It is hard to imagine how a hundred boats once worked these waters. (Simon Cooper Collection)

14ft in length, beamy with transom sterns. The frames were oak and the planking larch, and there were three thwarts and two rowing positions. They were painted inside and out with tar, from which the name Black Tar Point came, the traditional place of tarring. Rigged with a single lugsail sheeted through a hole in the heavy gunwale, this was used to sail downstream during the autumn herring season. For this, an anadromous herring that swam from the open sea into the freshwater river to spawn, drift-nets were set.

A closer view where, unusually, two men are in the boat. They are sitting on one side to counteract the weight of the suspended net. (Simon Cooper Collection)

Another view of the same boat where it is possible to see the line mooring the boat. (Simon Cooper Collection)

The river below Hook. The scene gives an impression of the absolute calmness of the upper reaches of the river. (Simon Cooper Collection)

Compass-net boats at anchor in 1999. Although they look the same, these are fibreglass boats. (Simon Cooper Collection)

A typical wooden compass-net boat. They were heavily built to withstand the stress of the net.

K6 at Llangwm. All the boats were registered and they are recognisable from the 'K' painted on the bow.

This boat was on the marsh by the river when I measured her up in about 1996 and drew up a lines plan. The two poles are the rimes of the compass net.

To compass-net for salmon they left the mast and sail ashore. The main fishing ground lay in the river at Little Milford below Hook on the Western Cleddau, yet the Llangwm men believed the rights to the fishing were their birthright as they'd been at it longer than the Hook folk. The majority of Hook men were employed in the local anthracite mine until its closure in 1947 but they persisted in stressing that they were geographically closest to Little Milford so had just as much right. However, with the Hook men being limited to fishing only the Western Cleddau and the Llangwm men being able to fish both rivers, it would appear that the authorities sided with the fishermen from Llangwm.

Like the stop-net, the compass-net consists of a bag net suspended between two 20ft larch poles. These poles, called rimes, are sourced locally and buried in the mud of the river for a few years to season. The boat is anchored across the flow of the river by attaching a warp between a stake on one side of the river and an anchor on the other. Once the boat is so positioned – he can move it across the river as the tide ebbs – and the net opened, the boat is rocked at an alarming rate from side to side until the weight of the stone counterbalancing the net is overcome and the net slides down into the water and the bottom of the poles stick into the mud of the riverbed. It is at this point that the method is at its most dangerous for, if there's too much tide beneath the boat or the river is too deep, then the boat would capsize and the fisherman could well drown, especially when fishing at night. Once the net is down the fisherman holds the three feeling strings attached to strategic positions on the net so that once a fish – a salmon, sewin or bass

K4 with her net clearly visible over the stern. However, this is not the same boat as in the previous picture even if both are K4. Obviously this is a newer boat and made from fibreglass. (Simon Cooper Collection)

Another similar view, this time of K7. Again it is a fibreglass boat. Sadly that is the tendency these days and only one wooden boat still fishes. (Simon Cooper Collection)

If all else fails with the fishing, you can always get the wife to take you for a gentle row around the river! However, I can count at least eight other similar boats in this photograph. (Mike Smylie Collection)

– strikes he feels this and immediately he heaves down on the head of the poles which close and the whole net comes down, hopefully with the fish still in the net. By the time of low water – they fish from about three hours after high tide – they prefer to be in the centre of the river.

The iron stakes are set into the riverbed and never change position and thus these determine the fishing stations, each with a name such as the Bite or the Grimbank. On the Eastern Cleddau two stakes are named Ormond and Edwards. In the middle of the nineteenth century there were seventy compass-net licences, though this had reduced to twenty-one in 1939. The fishing rota was decided at the beginning of the season and each man took his turn at the first stake, which is regarded as pole position. Today there are only eight and fishing is confined between 1 June and 31 August and prohibited between 6a.m. on Saturday to noon on Monday. Thus the season is short and the catches low and those that do continue do it first to keep the tradition alive and, secondly, they say to absorb the calm of the river for a few hours. Presumably the added bonus of the odd fish for the pot encourages a prolonged enthusiasm.

Alun Lewis is one fisherman who continues the tradition. He says that if he and the others don't that will be another rural skill disappeared forever. He first went out with his father when he was seven and went back to it ten years later. When he was about thirty-eight he took on his father's licence and intends to continue as long as possible, taking his son Gethin out at times and who he hopes will continue after he gives up. Furthermore he is the only one of today's fishermen to use a wooden tarred compass-net boat which has been passed down to him through several generations. The others all use fibreglass versions these days and unfortunately the numbers of the old wooden boats are depleting quickly. When I measured up a couple lying on the riverbank several years ago I suggested to one owner that he might sell his. The answer was a definite no for he preferred to see it rot away in front of his home. Thus these traditional boat types disappear forever, as do the skills that went hand in hand with the vessel. That, sadly, is the same story throughout Britain though fortunately here the few still persist with tradition, as does Stephen Perham in Clovelly. Thankfully, too, visitors today won't be met by a hail of stones on entry to Llangwm. Some things, like the invention of the wheel, do change for the best!

9

FROM HAKE TO HERRING – THE GROWTH OF THE PORT OF MILFORD

I n the 1920s Milford – we shall call it that following local tradition as I was informed – became the premier herring port in England and Wales, an astonishing achievement given the massive amount landed from the North Sea into East Anglia, with some of that herring being sent to the east coast in the peak year of 1925 to make up their shortfall. By the same year there were five smokehouses in Milford which ultimately caused local protests to the alleged nuisance caused by the excessive smoke. With over 200 steam drifters landing into the port this amount of smoke was considered justified by those fishermen and boat owners who asserted that any attempt to slow down the herring fisheries would lead to hardship amongst those inhabitants whose living depended on it. Three years later, however, a court case was held in Carmarthen at which three firms were accused of allowing 'offensive, poisonous and unwholesome smoke vapour' to issue from their premises. After three days of witness testimony, the judge found in favour of the firms and that those living in the town had to expect such inconveniences. No fishing port in Britain, it has been said, could 'turn a herring into a kipper quicker than at Milford'.

At the same time the port was one of four chief fishing ports of England and Wales, alongside Hull, Grimsby and Fleetwood. This was due to the volume of trawled fish – as against herring which was caught by drifters – being landed. However, a century earlier Milford was little more than a couple of farms and a chapel and even forty years before fishing was not what the founders had in mind when they planned their harbour.

An early ketch–rigged smack, this being the 58ft *Presto*, M18, built in the Isles of Scilly in 1860 and sold to Milford in 1866. She was eventually broken up in 1901. (Courtesy of Steve Farrow)

The first settlers, in 1793, were Quakers, whalers from Nantucket, Massachusetts, who were keen to develop a new centre for their whale oil activities which was already being sold to light London's streets. Hubberston and Hakin were, at that time, thriving centres of maritime activities in their own rights and these included shipbuilding, fishing, local trade and a packet service to Ireland. Although already contemplated, plans soon resurfaced in the early nineteenth century to build a town and port around Hubberston Pill but little was actually put into effect, largely due to the lack of funds. The operation was planned by Charles Grenville, nephew of the absentee landlord of the estate Sir William Hamilton who had inherited it from his deceased first wife. In the summer of 1802 Grenville invited Hamilton, his recent second wife Lady Emma and Lord Nelson, already a naval hero after his exploits at the Battle of the Nile, to visit Milford after the Hamiltons had been staying with Nelson at Merton Place, Surrey. The visit gave optimism to the developments, though Hamilton died the following year and Grenville in 1809. Grenville's brother Robert Fulke succeeded him as life-tenant of the estate,

A smaller Milford smack rigged with main, foresails and topsail and dried out within the harbour confines. Note the other smacks in the background. (Mike Smylie Collection)

Dominion, M27, a ketch-rigged smack built by Uphams of Brixham in 1903. She moved to Milford in 1909 and was sold to France in 1931. (Courtesy of Milford Haven Port Authority)

though he had little of his brother's drive. His wife was reputed to have said 'Milford had better remain as cornfields' and certainly they spent little time at the estate. However, he did appear at the annual regatta in August 1812 at which time he 'offered prizes for three classes of trawl boats employed bona fide as fishing boats in the Haven and belonging to it'. The prizes consisted of money and trawl nets which would be gratefully received by the fishermen. This is the first mention of trawl boats working in the waterway, though whether they were actually trawl boats or, as is more likely, drift-netters for herrings and/or oyster dredgers is uncertain. That the surrounding seas were rich in fish since

An early steam trawler *Fuchsia*, M127, alongside the ice factory and fish market. She was built by Edwards Brothers of North Shields and came to Milford in 1896 when she still had a ketch rig. She was captured by a German U-boat in 1916, the crew taken prisoner and the boat sunk. (Courtesy of John Stevenson)

The trawler *Essex*, M193, built in 1906 in North Shields and sold to Spain in 1925. (Courtesy of Fleetwood Maritime Heritage Trust)

The Castle Class side trawler *Milford Duchess*, built in South Shields as *James Gill*, in 1919 for the Admiralty. She fished from Fleetwood (at the time of this photo) and went to Milford in 1929. She was then requisitioned by the Admiralty between 1939 and 1944 and was eventually broken up in Dublin in 1952. (Courtesy of Fleetwood Maritime Heritage Trust)

The *Admiral Sir John Lawford* was built as an Icelandic Class trawler in Stockton-on-Tees in 1930. She first worked from Lowestoft and Fleetwood as LO42 (as in photo) although she was Fleetwood-owned until 1958 when she was purchased by the Milford Steam Trawling Co. in 1958. She was requisitioned from 1939 to 1946 for minesweeping operations and went to Normandy in 1944. She returned to Milford in 1946 and was broken up in 1962. (Courtesy of Fleetwood Maritime Heritage Trust)

Milford Docks about the end of the nineteenth century. Sailing smacks are still working though it appears the ice factory hasn't been built. (Courtesy of Tenby Museum)

Unloading Norwegian ice which was used to keep the fish fresh before the ice factory was built. (Scolton Manor Collection, Pembrokeshire Museum Service)

The first smoke house built at Milford Docks, 1905. (Scolton Manor Collection, Pembrokeshire Museum Service)

the seventeenth century is attested by George Owen in his *Description of Pembrokeshire*, first appearing in manuscript form in 1603 and later published in the last decade of the eighteenth century. Herring and oysters certainly appear to have been the principle fisheries of the waterway at the time. Owen informs us that, in 1602, the whole of the Pembrokeshire coast – from the Teifi to Amroth – was 'laid siege' to by huge shoals of herring which he described as God's blessing to 'this poor country'.

The town of Milford, situated between Hubberston and Castle Pills, did progress, albeit slowly, through the first half of the nineteenth century. Robert Fulke died in 1824 and his son Robert Fulke Murray took over but was seemingly as absent as his father. In 1831 he decided to fight the election of the sitting MP. His campaign was described as 'scandalous' after he tried buying votes en masse though he lost and eventually left the country.

A railway was planned between Manchester, through mid-Wales to Milford and an application provisionally lodged in 1845 by the Manchester & Milford Haven Railway Company. It was considered at the time that, due to the town's location between the pills, it would be a perfect position to construct a west coast deep water port which could attract the transatlantic trade. About 1851 the absentee landlord arrived home, although now as Colonel Grenville. He suddenly had great enthusiasm for the plans, until, however, Brunel's South Wales Railway arrived in Neyland in 1856. Neyland had been a fishing port since the previous century when, according to the 1758 Report on the British Fisheries, some 100,000 herrings were landed annually. With the terminus of

The ice factory, built next to the fish market in 1901. (Scolton Manor Collection, Pembrokeshire Museum Service)

Porters trundling fish boxes between two trains behind Milford's fish market, c.1919. (Scolton Manor Collection, Pembrokeshire Museum Service)

Trawlers at the fish market quay, early 1920s. (Scolton Manor Collection, Pembrokeshire Museum Service)

the railway, a ferry service to Ireland was soon introduced, this being a blow to Grenville's plans for his Milford. In 1863 the line was extended to Milford although the Manchester to Milford line was never completed. By the following year a foundation stone was laid amongst much pomp, though no work occurred afterwards. Ten years later, after Grenville's death in 1867, ownership passed to the trustees of The National Provident Institution which had been owed half a million pounds by Grenville.

Ten years after that first foundation stone was laid another was, after the Milford Docks Act came into force for the building works around Hubberston Pill. Work was supposed to be completed in six years but as with all the previous promises associated with Milford, it wasn't. The *Great Eastern* made an appearance in 1881 as a sort of publicity stunt though she later had to be towed out of the partially constructed dock. At that time the Haven was thriving with maritime traffic and the census shows over 150 vessels of British and Irish ownership as being berthed.

Once again it was the transatlantic trade that the directors of the Docks Company looked to. There were years of delays and setbacks, especially after the engineer Samuel Lake, having entered into a contract to build a deepened dock in eight months for £80,000, failed to do so and went bankrupt. Work ceased in 1882 and, with Hubberston Pill closed so that no shipbuilding could continue, associated businesses also closed and Milford was once again at an all-time low. New directors for the Docks Company were appointed and work on the dock commenced once again but only after a period of four years.

Above: Milford fish market in the 1930s. (Scolton Manor Collection, Pembrokeshire Museum Service)

Left: Milford Docks in the 1930s when the port was Britain's premier fish harbour. (Mike Smylie Collection)

Construction was finally completed in 1888, almost a century after Charles Grenville's original plans to 'make and provide quays, docks, piers and other erections and to establish a market with proper roads and avenues within the manor and lordship of Hubberston and Pill' were first put forward. But by this time it was too late, for Liverpool had built up a command of the transatlantic trade to Milford's disadvantage. The first vessel supposedly to enter the new dock, on 27 September 1888, was the steam trawler *Sybil*, LT77, although one informant suggested that in fact it was the smack *Children's Friend* that was first in. There is, however, no confirmation of this latter piece of information. Whichever it was,

The Dutch-built trawler *Mercurius*, FD277, and *Stephanie*, M177, lying alongside at Milford in 2010.

One of the original cranes on the dockside on Mackerel Quay.

The Cornish lugger FY221 in the marina. Being one of the only harbours where boats can stay afloat at all times, boats from all over the west coast use it.

The harbour during the annual Milford Fish Festival in 2010. This festival marks the beginning of a whole week of fish promotion in hotels and restaurants, organised by Pembrokeshire County Council.

to many it became obvious that the time was ripe to switch visions from the transatlantic business to that of the more local needs of the fishing industry. At first the answer from those with the reins appeared to be 'no'. When in the following year the *City of Rome* was persuaded to call in en route from America to Liverpool to drop off 134 passengers, amongst which were members of Barnum's Great American Circus, these passengers and their luggage were taken ashore by tender six miles from the dock because of the lack of a landing stage. The ensuing publicity should have alerted the directors to the desperation of their desire. Even in 1890, after more than 1,600 fishing vessels had entered the dock, did they still persist with their aim of attracting the American and Canadian ships. But it was to the fishing industry that Milford ultimately had to look to for its eventual prosperity and before long the directors just had to accept this. It is just that for ten years subsequent to the opening that they continued to press for transatlantic liners to call in.

Sailing trawlers from, primarily, Brixham and Lowestoft (as had been the *Children's Friend*) had been landing into the haven – especially Neyland – for many years, especially after the railway link to London – and thus the main fish market at Billingsgate – had been established. The Western Approaches were rich in fish yet had been only partially exploited, especially the supplies of hake off the southeast coast of Ireland. By the time the *Sybil* arrived from Lowestoft, trawler owners were already considering moving to Milford after realising the benefits of moving away from the recognised ports of Grimsby, Hull, Lowestoft, Yarmouth, Plymouth and Brixham. Fleetwood, to the north, was also experiencing a similar growth with rich pickings to the west of Scotland and out into the Northern Atlantic. The demand for hake also played a major part in the expansion of that fishing port.

By the beginning of the next year (1889), twelve fishing vessels were using the port and within a few years some fifty-five steam trawlers and 200 sailing smacks, yet the directors stuck to their guns and would not accept the obvious. New fishing craft were by this time being built locally. In Hakin, on the west side of the port, William Wolfe set up a yard and built the 20-ton, 56ft iron-built steam long-liner *Hit and Miss* for his own use as he also owned the two steam trawlers *Nile* and *Essex*.

When the volume of fish landed amounted to 18,245 tons in 1899 the directors had accepted their fate and began to provide facilities for the development of the dock as a major fishing port. Ice was imported from Norway until a purpose-made ice factory was built in one of the converted storage sheds originally built for the transatlantic trade. Another was converted into a fish market. Trains left for London and Cardiff loaded with fish. A second ice factory was built in 1901 when supply couldn't meet demand and even after this some ice continued to be imported. By 1904, 28,000 tons of mainly whitefish was being landed. The number of sailing smacks had decreased with an overall increase in the number of steam trawlers. Four years later landings were over 44,000 tons with Milford trawlers fishing as far off as Morocco.

The Fleetwood-based trawler *Jacinta*, FD159, that used to work from that port but is now a museum ship travelling to many festivals around the coasts. Visitors can view the ship and the exhibition showing the fishery.

In the first few years of the twentieth century pelagic fish (mackerel and herring) accounted for a substantial percentage of the fish landed and to satisfy this increase a new 'Herring Wharf' was built outside of the main dock so that the steam drifters could land at any state of the tide and not have to wait for the dock gates to open. In early 1905, seventy drifters were regularly using this wharf with its own market and smokehouse. By 1908 the new fish market was completed inside the dock, this being 950ft in length, one of the largest and most modern in Britain. It was at this time that Milford sat alongside Hull, Grimsby and Fleetwood as the major whitefish ports of England and Wales. By the beginning of the second decade of the century the sailing boats were motorised, some at Hancock's Milford Engineering and Ship Repairing Works where petrol/paraffin units by such names as Kelvin and Gardner were installed. Milford was, in all, experiencing an enterprising boom for all involved where they had the most up-to-date dock in Britain. To the fishermen and boat owners, the rope and sail makers, the engineers and ship repairers, the ice-makers, auctioneers and fish buyers 'fish was king' though it must be said that there was, at that time, the beginnings of a gradual decrease in the fortunes of the trawlers because of overfishing. Then, just as Sod's Law dictates, war broke out in 1914.

Fishing almost ceased overnight because, out of the seventy trawlers based in Milford, sixty were requisitioned by the Admiralty for duties which involved patrolling and mine sweeping. Many of these were subsequently sunk for, out of some 3,000 British fishing trawlers and drifters taken over by the Admiralty during the war, 376 were lost on active duty. Some boats continued fishing yet they, too, were sunk by enemy action (675 in total in Britain). In Milford the hole made in the fleet was partly compensated by the arrival of twenty-four Belgian trawlers with 700 refugees aboard, for these boats continued fishing throughout the war.

Fishing recommenced after the war in earnest and within a few years Milford was back to enjoying record catches. Almost 60,000 tons of fish were landed in 1917. Part of this consisted of vast amounts of herring which led to the five smokehouses being built and the subsequent court case. It was indeed the premier herring port with landings of over fifty million herring in 1922. At that time there were nearly 100 fish buyers in the town sending fish all over the country, mostly still by railway. There were three herring seasons: the Irish herring around Christmas, the spring herring off the Smalls in June and the summer herring between August and September. At other times local boats fished the North Sea, especially in the autumn after September. But again the whitefish landings were in decline and vessels were having to sail further and further afield to fill their holds.

In the 1920s it was estimated that some 1,200 Milford men worked aboard the Milford fleet at any one time. However, the 1926 general strike caused many trawler owners to go bust because they had bought vessels prior to the Depression at greatly inflated prices which could not be sustained afterwards. By the time of the fishermen's strike in 1932 over pay there were still 108 trawlers with another 150 boats using the port for several months a year. By the onset of the Second World War in 1939 Milford was suffering from overfishing and cheaper imports from, mainly, Spanish trawlers. Vessels were requisitioned once again and after peace in 1945 Milford never regained its fleet capacity. In 1953 there were still seventy-eight trawlers registered there though this declined to fourteen vessels by 1974.

Today's modern fishing boats are a lifetime away from their predecessors. This small boat, registered in Dundee, works lobster pots from Milford.

By 1991 most of the signs of a fishing industry of substance had been removed by the building of a marina. The fish market, smokehouses and ice factories were demolished. These were replaced with much smaller landing facilities on the west side and today most fish that passes through comes ashore from Belgian, French or Spanish trawlers and is loaded aboard refrigerated lorries and taken directly across to the continent. The electronic auction in the market was the first in the UK, so most of the selling is done whilst the vessels are still at sea. The original graving dock, which can accommodate ships up to 140m in length and 19m in width, is still in use by the Milford Haven Ship Repairers which in turn is an offshoot of the Milford Haven Port Authority.

The harbour front is also still alive. Pembrokeshire College offer courses in marine engineering, boatbuilding and design and some students come from the fishing industry on a part-time basis. Nearby, as part of the 'Rising Tide' initiative to connect Celtic communities, young students are building a replica Tenby Lugger in a purpose-built facility overlooking the harbour. The aim is to strengthen ties between Wales and Ireland with the intervening sea as the common ground. Interpretation and preservation of the maritime culture is the main goal and hence the training aspect whilst they also aim to encourage community regeneration through assisting in local maritime festivals. However Milford, upholding the tradition that 'fish is king', has hosted a fish festival in June for several years as part of the Pembrokeshire Fish Week in which, for the whole seven days, fish is promoted throughout the county. This must be a unique event which doesn't need much assistance which just goes to show that inshore fishing is still very much alive in Pembrokeshire. 'Kipperland' made its debut there in 2009, smoking herring on the quayside for the first time in many years. All in all, reminders of the once great industry that the town was built upon in the twentieth century are long gone, though some of Milford's inhabitants, drawn by my smokehouse, recalled the good times of working in the smokehouses and how beef fat was sold to the visiting boats. One fellow told me how his grandfather was the 'kipper inspector', a sort of modern-day quality controller, while another recounted how his father had opened the vents on the smokehouse during the night; all stories from the past. Today's Milford does seem a bit of a mismatch in some ways, though not to the same extent as Fleetwood. The Victorian buildings higher up stare down upon the modern cluster of buildings and gleaming plastic yachts in and around the marina and the 'new' developments on the east side of the dock. Although they have retained the name, Mackerel Quay is largely a car park but otherwise, like many other seaside towns that once relied upon fishing for their development, it seems today's town elders are just as keen to banish that particular memory as were the founders back in the 1880s when they regarded the 'despised fishing trade' with contempt. To them it was an odious and unwelcome presence, bringing rat infestations and people of a low character. After all, what were these vile people compared to the passengers aboard ocean-going liners? Ironic, isn't it, that these same folk had to eventually eat their own words and let the fishing boats in!

One group not to have to eat their words is the Milford Haven Fishing Industry Memorial Group which is actively recruiting support from those with family links to the fishing industry – at sea or ashore – to fund and construct a memorial to all those relatives and others who worked to create the industry. At first this will be a temporary memorial until redevelopment around the entrance to the harbour is complete, after which a permanent garden and sculptures can be commissioned. Plaques commemorating those who lost their lives are also planned. Finally, for those interested in discovering more about the boats that worked from here, the website of the Milford Steam Trawlers (see Bibliography) is a must.

BIBLIOGRAPHY

Edwards, Sybil	*The Story of the Milford Haven Waterway*, Almeley, 2001
Farr, Grahame	*Ships and Harbours of Exmoor*, Dulverton, 1970
Gilman, John	*Exmoor's Maritime Heritage*, Dulverton, 1999
Grant, A. and Waters, P.	*Salmon Netting in North Devon*, Appledore, 1998
James, T.	*Yankee Jack Sails Again: A Sentimental Journey to the Forgotten Ports of the Southwest*, Suffolk, 2006
Jenkins, J.G.	*The Inshore Fishermen of Wales*, Cardiff, 1991
March, E.J.	*Inshore Craft of Great Britain* (vol. 2), Barnsley, 2005
Matheson, Colin	*Wales and the Sea Fisheries*, Cardiff, 1929
Owen, George	*The Description of Pembrokeshire*, Llandysul, 1994
Rees, J.F.	*The Story of Milford*, Cardiff, 1957
Smylie, M.	*The Herring Fishers of Wales*, Llanrwst, 1998
–	*Traditional Fishing Boats of Britain & Ireland*, Shrewsbury, 1999
–	*Herring – A History of the Silver Darlings*, Stroud, 2004
–	*Working the Welsh Coast*, Stroud, 2005
Stuckey, P.J.	*The Sailing Pilots of the Bristol Channel*, Bristol, 1999
Taylor, J.N.	*Fishing on the Lower Severn*, Gloucester, 1974
Waters, Brian	*Severn Tide*, London, 1947
–	*The Bristol Channel*, London, 1955

WEBSITES

Fleetwood Maritime Heritage Trust	www.fmht.co.uk
Milford Haven Port Authority	www.mhpa.co.uk
Milford Steam Trawlers	www.milfordtrawlers.org.uk
Pembrokeshire Virtual Museum	www.pembrokeshirevirtualmuseum.co.uk

158

Other titles published by The History Press

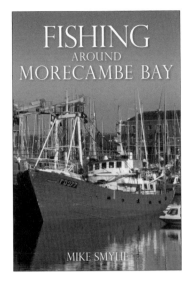

Fishing Around Morecambe Bay
MIKE SMYLIE

Mike Smylie takes the reader on a wonderfully comprehensive journey through the history of fishing in and around Morecambe Bay in this first book to be devoted to fishing in the locale. It spans a wide area covering places such as Barrow, Ulverston, Grange-over-Sands, Morecambe, Glasson and Fleetwood. It covers a wide variety of topics – from salmon and shrimps to Lancashire nobbies and fishing on horseback – ensuring there is something of interest to everyone.

Featuring over 170 photographs, this book is packed full of interesting facts, such as the use of horses to drag trawl-nets through shallow waters – a practice unique to the British coast. Recounting the history of the fisheries by boat, horse and hand, *Fishing around Morecambe Bay* is sure to appeal to both fishing industry enthusiasts and those with an interest in the history of the local area.

978-0-7524-5393-4

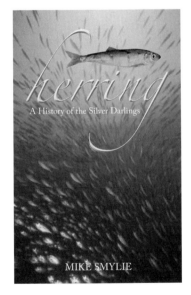

Herring – A History of the Silver Darlings
MIKE SMYLIE

The story of herring is entwined in the history of commercial fishing. For over two millennia, herring have been commercially caught and its importance to the coastal peoples of Britain cannot be measured. At one point tens of thousands were involved in the catching, processing and sale of herring. They followed the shoals around the coast from Stornoway to Penzance and many towns on Britain's east coast grew rich on the backs of the 'silver darlings'. Fishing expert Mike Smylie looks at the effects of the herring on the people who caught them, the unique ways of life, the superstitions of boats and communities who lived for the silver darlings.

With a wealth of illustrations, this fascinating book reveals the little-known history of the herring. And for those who've neglected the silver darlings for lesser fish such as cod and haddock, there are a number of mouth-watering recipes to try.

978-0-7524-5951-6

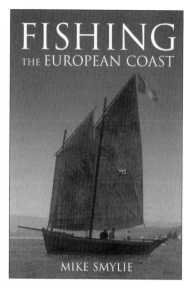

Fishing the European Coast
MIKE SMYLIE

No one knows when the first fishing boat set out to sea, although river fishing by boat was quite likely the earlier. Mosaics from the Mediterranean show vessels encircling shoals dating from the first century, although Egyptian tomb reliefs dated to 6000BC show nets being set. In Britain we also know that Mesolithic man was moving about by boat, again in about 6000BC. These people, primarily wanderers, were also hunter gatherers. Jesus, we are told, sailed aboard fishing boats on the Sea of Galilee around the early years of the first century AD, whilst Caesar noted that wooden boats were in use in Britain sometime after the Roman invasion. However, within these pages, it is really only the last two centuries that concern us. Although the roots of some of the vessels may go back many generations, in the main those in this book are still in existence in some form or other, even if not for their original intended use.

978-0-7524-4628-8

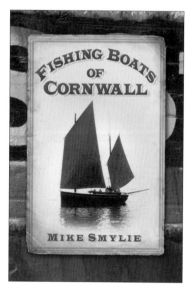

Fishing Boats of Cornwall
MIKE SMYLIE

The first deep-sea fishing boats of Cornwall are regarded as being influenced by the three-masted French luggers that sailed over to cause havoc amongst the locals. However, fishing had been practised by Cornishmen for many generations before that, with mackerel and pilchard fishing being prominent. Inshore, lobster and crab fishing had also been popular for generations. This book looks at the development of Cornish fishing boats, from the lugger to Pilchard seine-net boats, and traditional lobster and crab vessels. These are discussed alongside more unusual boats, such as the St Ives 'jumbo' and the Mevagissey 'tosher'. The book brings the story up to date, including modern photos of existing boats gathering for the bi-annual Looe lugger regatta. After motorisation, the shape of the boat changed forever and the adaptation of old boats to accommodate engines is examined, as are the famous yards and boatbuilders of Cornwall still operational today.

978-0-7524-4906-7